Ius Comparatum – Global Studies in Comparative Law

Volume 29

More information about this series at http://www.springer.com/series/11943

Académie internationale de droit comparé
International Academy of Comparative Law

Katharina Boele-Woelki •
Diego P. Fernàndez Arroyo
Editors

The Past, Present and Future of Comparative Law - Le passé, le présent et le futur du droit comparé

Ceremony of 15 May 2017 in Honour of 5 Great Comparatists - Cérémonie du 15 mai 2017 en l'honneur de 5 grands comparatistes

Éditeur assistant/Assistant Editor: Alexandre Senegacnik

Springer

Editors
Katharina Boele-Woelki
International Academy of
Comparative Law
Paris, France

Diego P. Fernàndez Arroyo
International Academy of Comparative Law
Paris, France

ISSN 2214-6881 ISSN 2214-689X (electronic)
Ius Comparatum – Global Studies in Comparative Law
ISBN 978-3-030-06719-9 ISBN 978-3-319-93770-0 (eBook)
https://doi.org/10.1007/978-3-319-93770-0

This Springer imprint is published by the registered company Springer Nature Switzerland AG
The registered company address is: Gewerbestrasse 11, 6330 Cham, Switzerland

Préface/Preface

Préface

Le 15 mai 2017, l'Académie internationale de droit comparé a rendu hommage à cinq grands comparatistes. C'était la première fois dans l'histoire de l'Académie qu'un tel événement a été organisé, et il a eu lieu à Paris.

Les noms des illustres comparatistes sont connus de tous ceux qui ont déjà foulé le magnifique terrain du droit comparé : Jean-Louis BAUDOUIN du Canada, Xavier BLANC-JOUVAN de France, Mary Ann GLENDON des États-Unis d'Amérique, Hein D. KÖTZ d'Allemagne, et Rodolfo SACCO d'Italie.

Pour l'occasion, ils ont été invités à donner leurs visions sur « le passé, le présent et le futur du droit comparé ». Le contenu des contributions de nos invités était si riche que l'idée de préparer un ouvrage s'est instantanément imposée. Pour l'évènement à Paris, une discussion ouverte a été préférée à la place d'une succession traditionnelle de discours. Ainsi, en table ronde, les échanges sur le passé, le présent et le futur du droit comparé ont été organisés autour de trois

Preface

On 15 May 2017, the International Academy of Comparative Law paid tribute to five great comparatists. This was the first time in the history of the Academy that such an event was held, and it took place in Paris.

The names of the outstanding comparatists are well known by anyone who has ever set foot in the magnificent field of comparative law: Jean-Louis BAUDOUIN from Canada, Xavier BLANC-JOUVAN from France, Mary Ann GLENDON from the United States, Hein D. KÖTZ from Germany and Rodolfo SACCO from Italy.

On this occasion, they were asked to give their visions about "the past, the present and future of comparative law". The content of our guest's contributions was so valuable that the idea of compiling a book immediately arose. For the event in Paris, an open discussion was preferred over a traditional sequence of speeches. Thus, in the roundtable, the exchanges about the past, the present and the future of comparative law were organised around three topics: (1) the

thémes : (1) l'avenir de l'Académie internationale de droit comparé, (2) la méthodologie du droit comparé, et (3) l'enseignement du droit comparé. Nous pouvons dire que nous avons assisté à deux heures de divertissement intellectuel du plus haut niveau.

Près de 200 personnes du monde entier ont assisté à l'évènement. Étant donné que l'Académie rendait hommage à ces cinq personnalités académiques, le public devait d'abord comprendre pourquoi le Bureau de l'Académie les avait choisies pour cette cérémonie. Qu'ont précisément apporté ces cinq savants ? Pourquoi sont-ils si bien connus ? Qu'ont-ils offert au droit comparé ? En quoi diffèrent-ils, et quand et pourquoi ont-ils excellé ? Beaucoup dans le public connaissaient les réponses à ces questions; cependant, elles ont été rappelées par cinq autres comparatistes du droit entretenant des liens privilégiés et de longue date avec nos invités d'honneur : Marta CARTABIA d'Italie, Bénédicte FAUVARQUE-COSSON de France, Antonio GAMBARO d'Italie, Attila HARMATHY de Hongrie et Marek SAFJAN de Pologne. Leurs cinq éloges ont été suivis de brèves réponses de nos célébrités du droit comparé, qui se sont alors immédiatement engagées dans un riche débat modéré par la Présidente de l'Académie.

Les trois sujets choisis sont non seulement susceptibles de présenter le débat parmi les Maestros, mais en outre, ils représentent les moyens par lesquels nous souhaitons développer les réflexions sur le rôle de l'Académie afin de faire face aux défis actuels du droit comparé. Plusieurs questions spécifiques sont en jeu, comme suit.

future of the International Academy of Comparative Law, (2) comparative law methodology and (3) teaching comparative law. We can say that we were treated to two hours of high-level intellectual entertainment.

Almost 200 people from all around the world attended the event. Given that the Academy was paying tribute to the five legal scholars, the audience first had to understand why the Executive Committee of the Academy had selected them for this ceremony. What precisely have these five scholars achieved? Why are they so very well known? What have they contributed to comparative law? How do they differ, and when and why did they excel? Many of those at the event knew the answers to these questions; however, they were concisely recalled by five other legal comparatists with long-standing ties with our honoured guests: Marta CARTABIA from Italy, Bénédicte FAUVARQUE-COSSON from France, Antonio GAMBARO from Italy, Attila HARMATHY from Hungary and Marek SAFJAN from Poland. Their five eulogies were followed by brief replies delivered by our celebrities of comparative law, who then immediately engaged into a rich debate moderated by the President of the Academy.

The three selected topics are not only apt to introduce the debate among the Maestros. Furthermore, they represent the avenues by means of which we intend to develop the reflections about the role of the Academy in order to cope with the current challenges of comparative law. Several specific issues are at stake, as follows.

1 L'Avenir de l'Académie Internationale de droit Comparé

Penser l'avenir d'une institution en passe d'achever son premier siècle d'existence peut sembler audacieux. Il est sans doute plus facile de scruter son passé. Néanmoins, notre Académie demeure indéniablement attrayante pour de nombreux juristes. Ainsi, les listes de candidatures pour le titre de membre associé demeurent qualitativement et quantitativement bien fournies. On peut penser que, même s'ils peuvent être séduits par le passé prestigieux de l'Académie, la majorité des candidats est également confiante dans ce que l'Académie peut réaliser dans le futur.

Nonobstant les forces de notre organisation, il y a aussi certainement des faiblesses. La plus importante de ces dernières est peut-être le fait que d'autres associations mondiales, régionales et nationales ont « découvert » l'approche comparative. Elles sont entrées dans notre domaine, et on pourrait dire qu'elles sont en quelque sorte en concurrence avec nos activités. La question qui se pose dans cette perspective est de savoir si nous pouvons offrir quelque chose de différent des autres. En principe, il doit y avoir de la place pour nous tous. Néanmoins, nous remarquons que de nombreux spécialistes dans divers domaines ne sont pas engagés avec notre Académie, mais plutôt avec des organisations plus spécifiques et leurs propres événements. Cette situation pourrait être considérée comme une menace. Nous préférons y voir un défi qui devrait nous conduire à imaginer des activités plus diverses, attirant le plus grand nombre de juristes et – pourquoi pas – de spécialistes venant d'autres domaines scientifiques.

1 The Future of the International Academy of Comparative Law

Thinking about the future of an institution which is close to completing its first century of existence may appear as audacious. It is doubtlessly easier to scrutinise its past. However, our Academy undeniably remains attractive for many jurists. Thus, the lists of candidates for associate membership remain quantitatively and qualitatively well furnished. One may think that, although they may be appealed by the prestigious Academy's past, the majority of the candidates are also confident in what the Academy can achieve in the future.

Despite the strengths of our organisation, there are of course also weaknesses. Perhaps the most significant of the latter is represented by the fact that other global, regional and national societies have "discovered" the comparative approach. They have entered our domain, and one might say they are somehow competing with our activities. The question which arises from this perspective is whether we can offer something different than the others. In principle, there should be sufficient room for all of us. Nevertheless, we are noticing that many specialists in various fields are not engaged with our Academy but rather with more specific organisations and their own events. This situation might be seen as a threat. We prefer to see it as a challenge that should lead us to imagine more diverse activities appealing for the largest array of jurists and—why not—of specialists coming from other scientific fields.

Jusqu'à présent, nos activités ont consisté en des congrès généraux qui ont lieu tous les quatre ans. Depuis 1950, date du troisième congrès général, la fréquence de quatre ans n'a pas été interrompue. En outre, des congrès thématiques sont organisés entre deux congrès généraux depuis 2008. Ils ne durent que deux jours et demi, alors que les congrès généraux se déroulent sur une semaine.

So far, our activities have consisted of general congresses which take place every four years. Since 1950, when the third general congress was held, the four-year frequency has not been interrupted. In addition, since 2008, thematic congresses are organised in between two general congresses. They last only two days and a half, whereas the general congresses take place over a week.

Devrions-nous continuer à organiser ce genre de manifestations ? Sont-elles toujours le moyen le plus efficace d'expérimenter et de pratiquer le droit comparé dans notre monde numérique d'aujourd'hui, dans lequel nous nous connectons facilement en quelques secondes ? À notre avis, la réponse est claire. Les livres électroniques et l'offre massive de tous les types de journaux électroniques ne sont pas parvenus à tuer les publications sur papier. De même, les moyens de communication en ligne ne remplaceront pas totalement – au moins pour un temps – les réunions au cours desquelles chaque participant pourra interagir directement avec les autres. Il s'ensuit que la piste à suivre semble être la quête d'une combinaison optimale de moyens permettant de réunir tous les membres de l'Académie.

Should we continue to organise this kind of conferences? Are they still the most effective way of experiencing and practising comparative law in our digitalised world of today, in which we easily connect within seconds? In our opinion, the answer is clear. E-books and the massive offer of e-journals of all types have not been able to kill the traditional on-paper publications. Online means of communication will not totally replace—at least for a while—the meetings in which every attendant can interact directly with each other. Then, the avenue to follow seems to be a quest for the optimal combination of means to get together all the members of the Academy.

S'agissant de la manière dont nos congrès sont organisés, la majorité des sujets a traditionnellement été abordée selon une méthodologie particulière : des sujets sont proposés et sélectionnés lors d'une réunion avec les représentants des comités nationaux. Un ou une rapporteur général est alors nommé(e) qui rédige un

With regard to the way in which our congresses are organised, traditionally the majority of the topics have been addressed according to a particular methodology: topics are proposed and selected at a meeting with representatives of the national committees. A general rapporteur is then appointed and

questionnaire auquel les rapporteurs nationaux répondent. Un rapport général est enfin rédigé sur la base des rapports nationaux. Nous pensons que cette méthodologie demeure utile et pertinente sur certaines questions mais qu'elle devrait être combinée avec d'autres, en particulier avec des ateliers interactifs.

De plus, l'utilisation de la méthodologie traditionnelle ne devrait pas se limiter à l'étude des systèmes juridiques nationaux, mais tenir compte de toute autre manifestation juridique, tels que les traités internationaux, le droit non étatique, les initiatives scientifiques, ainsi que les décisions nationales, internationales, supranationales ou transnationales. Il va sans dire que la prise en considération de facteurs non juridiques et l'extension de la comparaison au-delà du strict domaine juridique est également souhaitable. Dans ce contexte, la possibilité de créer un groupe de travail visant à réformer les congrès de l'Académie a également été évoquée.

Bien sûr, l'Académie n'est pas empêchée d'imaginer et de mettre en œuvre d'autres activités en dehors des congrès généraux et thématiques. Ainsi, deux démarches ont été initiées. La première consiste à organiser des événements spécifiques ayant un objet particulier (cet événement en étant un exemple évident) ou au sujet d'une thématique comparative spécifique. La seconde concerne l'enseignement et la erche, en offrant des programmes thématiques de droit comparé en association avec des institutions

he or she drafts a questionnaire which is answered by national rapporteurs. A general report is then drafted on the basis of these national reports. We do think that this methodology can remain useful and relevant for some specific issues but that it should be combined with other ones, particularly with interactive workshops.

Furthermore, the use of the traditional methodology should not be confined to the study of national legal systems but should also take into account any other legal manifestation, such as international treaties, non-State law, scientific initiatives as well as decisions of national, international, supranational or transnational origin. Needless to say that taking into consideration non-legal factors and expanding the comparison beyond the strict legal field would be also desirable. Within this context, the possibility to set up a working group aimed at reforming the Academy's congresses has also been evoked.

Of course, the Academy is not prevented to imagine and implement other activities besides the general and thematic congresses. In this vein, two lines of action have been initiated. The first one consists in organising specific events with either a particular purpose (this event being a clear example) or on a specific comparative theme. The second one deals with teaching and researching, by offering thematic programmes of comparative law in association with academic institutions,

académiques, de préférence avec des personnes morales. Concrètement, un premier programme pour doctorants est organisé avec le Max Planck Institute Luxembourg for International, European and Regulatory Procedural Law.

preferably with the Academy's corporate members. Concretely, a first programme for Ph.D. candidates is being organised together with the Max Planck Institute Luxembourg for International, European and Regulatory Procedural Law.

Quelle que soit l'activité, l'Académie vise à aborder les questions d'actualité les plus pertinentes en droit. Notre défi est d'améliorer les mécanismes utilisés pour sélectionner ces sujets afin de pouvoir identifier les plus pertinents et nécessaires.

Whichever the activity can be, the Academy aims to address the most topical and relevant issues in law. Our challenge is to improve the mechanisms used so far to select these topics in order to be able to identify the most appropriate and necessary.

2 Méthodologie du droit comparé

En ce qui concerne la méthodologie du droit comparé, plusieurs problèmes peuvent être soulignés.

2 Comparative Law Methodology

Coming to comparative law methodology, several issues can be pointed out.

Tout d'abord, même les comparatistes ont parfois du mal à apprécier l'aspect comparatiste d'une recherche juridique. En réalité, il est bien connu qu'il existe différents points de vue en ce qui concerne la détermination des exigences à remplir pour qu'une recherche particulière puisse être considérée comme comparative. En outre, selon certains chercheurs, la méthode comparative à utiliser dépend du domaine juridique dans lequel la recherche est menée. Nous sommes plus enclins à penser que, nonobstant certains éléments particuliers propres à chaque domaine juridique, il est possible d'établir un cadre méthodologique général pour tous les domaines du droit. L'Académie devrait fournir les outils pour élaborer un tel cadre.

First of all, even comparatists struggle sometimes to appreciate the comparative aspect of a given legal research. In fact, it is well known that there are different views to determine the most important threshold requirements to be fulfilled in order for a particular research to be considered comparative. In addition, according to some scholars, the comparative method to be used depends on the area of law in which the research is conducted. We are more inclined to believe that, notwithstanding the particular elements which remain specific to each legal field, it is nevertheless possible to establish a general methodological framework for all areas of the law. The Academy should provide the tools to elaborate such framework.

Deuxièmement, en tant que juristes, nous suggérons généralement que le droit doit être amélioré. En réalité, nous considérons que la partie la plus excitante de toute étude juridique comparative survient lorsque les différentes et possibles réformes du droit sont évaluées. D'autres ne sont pas d'accord. Ils pensent que cette dernière étape est uniquement la tâche des politiciens ou d'autres décideurs. Où se situent les membres de l'Académie dans cette discussion ? Quelle que soit la position de chacun, la discussion sur le rôle des comparatistcs sur ce point mériterait d'être ouverte.

Enfin nous savons que dans les faits l'obtention d'un soutien financier pour la recherche juridique – ce que l'on appelle le « revenu provenant du troisième courant » – exige en définitive une approche comparative ou multidisciplinaire. Ce sont les exigences générales des organismes de financement, qu'il s'agisse d'organisations internationales ou supranationales (comme l'Union européenne), de programmes de recherche ou de programmes d'organismes de financement nationaux. De plus en plus, cependant, ces deux approches doivent être combinées. Il faut non seulement mener une recherche juridique comparative, mais désormais également intégrer un élément de recherche économique ou sociologique. Cette approche nécessite un nombre énorme de compétences, mais n'est qu'une face de la médaille. L'autre face est constitutuée de contraintes de temps et d'accessibilité des données. C'est sans aucun doute un autre sujet de préoccupation pour nous en tant qu'importante institution académique.

Secondly, as legal scholars, we generally suggest that the law must be improved. In fact, we consider that the most exciting part of any comparative legal study arises when the various possible law-reform solutions are evaluated. Others disagree. They think this final step is only the task of politicians or other deciders. Where do the Academy's members stand in this discussion? Irrespectively of the position of each one, the very discussion about the role of the comparatists concerning this point would deserve to be open.

Finally, as a matter of fact, we know that nowadays obtaining financial support for legal research—the so-called third-stream income—ultimately requires either a comparative or a multidisciplinary approach. These are the general requirements of funding organisations, be they international or supranational organisations (like the European Union), research programmes or programmes of national funding organisations. Increasingly, however, both approaches need to be combined. Not only must comparative legal research be carried out, but an economic or sociological research element is now expected. This approach requires an enormous number of skills, but is only one side of the coin. The other side consists of time constraints and accessibility of data. This is, without any shadow of doubt, another particular concern for us as a major academic institution.

3 Enseigner le droit comparé

Si l'Académie elle-même et la méthodologie du droit comparé sont importants pour nous et requièrent des définitions claires pour tout futur projet, les aspects liés à l'enseignement n'en sont pas moins significatifs. En fait, l'internationalisation croissante de l'éducation juridique joue aujourd'hui un rôle clé dans l'avancement de la méthode juridique comparative. La connaissance d'autres systèmes juridiques peut être obtenue en étudiant à l'étranger et en suivant des cours portant sur des questions juridiques internationales et régionales. Quid de l'approche comparative dans l'éducation juridique ? Qu'est-ce que cela implique, et comment cela doit-il être mis en œuvre ? L'Académie ne devrait pas être absente de ce débat crucial.

Dans de nombreuses facultés de droit autour du globe – bien qu'elles ne soient pas majoritaires – il existe des cours de droit comparé. En tant qu'institution principale de ce domaine, l'Académie a plus qu'un mot à dire sur le contenu des enseignements de droit comparé. Nous nous demandons si un aperçu des différentes familles légales dans le monde devrait nous satisfaire. La réponse doit être négative. Les vastes connaissances sur les juridictions étrangères et leurs principales caractéristiques sont nécessaires mais en aucun cas suffisantes. Les possibilités de *l'Auslandsrechtskunde* sont souvent assez limitées. Pour compenser ces limites, nous devrions principalement nous concentrer sur la méthode. En réalité, la principale contribution que les autres chercheurs en droit attendent de nous est la réponse à la question « comment comparer ? ».

3 Teaching Comparative Law

If the Academy itself and the comparative law methodology are important to us and require clear definitions for any future project, the aspects related to teaching are not less significant. In fact, the growing internationalisation of legal education plays today a key role in advancing the comparative legal method. Knowledge of other legal systems can be acquired through studying abroad and following courses which address international and regional legal questions. What about the comparative approach in legal education? What does it entail, and how should it be implemented? The Academy should not be absent in this crucial debate.

In many law schools around the globe—although by far not the majority—there are courses on comparative law. As the main institution in this field, the Academy has more than a word to say about the content of comparative law curricula. We wonder if providing an overview of the various legal families in the world should satisfy us. The answer must be negative. The broad knowledge about foreign jurisdictions and their main features is necessary but by no means sufficient. The possibilities of the *Auslandsrechtskunde* are often quite limited. To compensate these limitations, we should principally focus on the method. In reality, the main contribution other legal researchers are expecting from us is the answer to the question "how to compare?"

Enfin, si nous regardons nos collègues plus jeunes, nous pouvons observer que peu d'entre eux prêtent attention au droit comparé. Ils n'aiment pas suivre une méthodologie de droit comparé. Ils semblent plus conscients de la critique de la méthodologie traditionnelle (prise consciemment ou inconsciemment comme « *mainstrea* ») que de la nécessité d'incorporer une touche comparatiste dans leur recherche. On trouve difficilement une démarche comparative dans leur travaux : rédiger un questionnaire, détecter les similitudes et les différences, tenter de les expliquer et évaluer les solutions. Au lieu de cela, ils préfèrent sélectionner et choisir. Ici et là, ils incluent des informations sur d'autres juridictions.

Finally, when we look at our younger fellows, we can observe that only few of them pay attention to comparative law. They do not like to follow a comparative law methodology. They seem more aware of the criticism about traditional methodology (consciously or unconsciously taken as "mainstream") than of the necessity to incorporate a comparative drop in their research. One can hardly find in their works a comparative process: drafting a questionnaire, detecting similarities and differences, making an attempt to explain them and evaluating the solutions. Instead, they prefer to pick and choose. Here and there, they include some information about other jurisdictions.

Nous pensons que l'Académie pourrait proposer des instruments pour traiter du droit comparé plus systématiquement. Ce faisant, nous encouragerions les jeunes chercheurs à se pencher sérieusement sur le droit comparé, ce qui pourrait en fin de compte avoir un impact positif sur l'amélioration des productions doctrinales en général.

We think that the Academy could offer the instruments to deal with comparative law more systematically. In doing so, we would encourage young scholars to deal seriously with comparative law, which ultimately could have a positive impact on the improvement of legal scholarship in general.

En plus d'un hommage largement mérité en raison de la hauteur scientifique de nos invités, l'hommage de l'Académie est un acte de justice. Beaucoup parmi la vaste communauté de droit comparé peuvent se distancer du contenu des apports doctrinaux de nos cinq honorés. Leurs idées et même la manière dont ils ont conçu l'utilisation de la méthodologie comparative ne sont assurément pas partagées par tout le monde. Nous croyons cependant que personne ne

In addition to a tribute broadly deserved on the basis of the scientific level of our guests, the Academy's celebration constitutes an act of justice. Many among the vast comparative law community may differ with the content of our honoured five's scholarship. Their ideas and even the way in which they have conceived the use of comparative methodology are surely not shared by everyone. We do believe, however, that nobody questions their attachment to

doute de leur attachement au droit comparé. Et cette dévotion d'une vie à l'étude comparative est en soi quelque chose à reconnaître.

comparative law. And this lifetime devotion to comparative studies is in itself something to recognise.

Paris, France Katharina Boele-Woelki
Paris, France Diego P. Fernàndez Arroyo

Table des matiéres / Contents

Partie I / Part I
Mary Ann Glendon

Reflection on the Comparative Study of Law in the 21st Century

Mary Ann Glendon

1 Comparative Law at a Crossroads

To legal scholars who have devoted much of their professional lives to the comparative study of legal systems, the benefits of comparative law can seem abundant, obvious, and more relevant than ever in today's increasingly globalized world. Yet, paradoxically, it is not at all clear what role cross-national legal studies will play in twenty-first century legal academies. Unprecedented global interdependence has spurred many changes in the standard law school curriculum, with course offerings proliferating in the areas of international business, international tax, international arbitration, public international law, and international human rights. These very changes, however, have fostered a mentality that is somewhat impatient with national, regional and local differences. To ardent proponents of standardized and universal norms, the comparative enterprise can seem unnecessary or obstructive. At the same time, persons concerned about globalization's disruptive effects on local cultures are apt to view foreign law studies with the same skepticism they hold toward internationalism in general.

Both of those attitudes are perhaps more prevalent in the United States where comparative legal studies were never as firmly established as in Europe. Like Roman jurists of old, many American lawyers are chauvinistically convinced that their legal and political arrangements do not need instruction from elsewhere.[1] Most

[1]On the relative indifference of Roman lawyers to comparative law, see Zweigert and Kötz (1998), p. 49.

M. A. Glendon (✉)
Harvard University, Cambridge, MA, USA
e-mail: glendon@law.harvard.edu

K. Boele-Woelki, D. P. Fernàndez Arroyo (eds.), *The Past, Present and Future of Comparative Law - Le passé, le présent et le futur du droit comparé*, Ius Comparatum – Global Studies in Comparative Law 29, https://doi.org/10.1007/978-3-319-93770-0_1

U.S. practitioners are still able to carry on their work without casting their eyes beyond national borders, and most legal scholars, with some notable exceptions, have been content to confine their comparative efforts to the study of the laws of the several states.

While France and Germany have had flourishing comparative law associations since the nineteenth century, it was not until 1951 that the American Association for the Comparative Study of Law was founded through the combined efforts of a handful of scholars who had fled Europe in the 1930s and with a few American lawyers who specialized in handling foreign transactions. Happily, that organization is much larger today, but when I joined in the early 1970s, it was still a small band of about a dozen Americans and a dozen elderly European emigrés.

No wonder that the legal changes stimulated by the acceleration of globalization seemed at first like a dream come true to American comparatists. Firms that used to regard study abroad as evidence of dilettantism began aggressively recruiting young lawyers who could communicate easily with their counterparts elsewhere and who could be persuasive in foreign settings. Law schools hastened to meet student demands for course offerings that would prepare them for professional life in a shrinking world. A few Supreme Court Justices occasionally referred to foreign law to bolster their decisions in high-profile cases. A close look at the expanded international programs in American law schools, however, reveals that there are still relatively few opportunities for the systematic study of comparative and foreign law.

On the supposition that a similar situation may exist—though to a lesser degree—in countries where comparative law has long had a stronger foothold, this seems like an opportune moment to reflect on what role comparative legal studies may have to play in a world where universalizing impulses push in one direction and movements for protection of local identities and autonomy pull in another.

2 What Comparatists Do and Why They Do It

Since even our fellow law professors sometimes ask what exactly it is that we do when we say we engage in the comparative study of law, let us begin by dispelling the notion, sometimes asserted, that comparative law is a distinctive method for conducting research. Legal scholars who work with foreign law are no different from their counterparts in the other human sciences who take for granted that serious research ought to include a comparative dimension. We thus count among our forebears Émile Durkheim, who maintained that "comparative sociology is not a particular branch of sociology; it is sociology itself,"[2] and Frederic Maitland who

[2]Durkheim (1966), p. 139.

insisted that the lawyer "who knew nothing or cared nothing for any system but his own hardly came in sight of the idea of legal history."[3]

Research in law, as in any other field, is a continuous process of asking questions, acquiring and attending to data, forming and testing hypotheses, and arriving at conclusions to be re-examined in the light of new data. In the natural sciences and in some social sciences, hypotheses are normally tested by experiments. But since controlled experimentation in law is hardly ever possible, an important feature of comparative law is that it expands our theater of observation, enabling us to see how other legal systems have dealt with problems similar to the ones we are studying. Along the way, we often become aware of questions that would not otherwise have occurred to us, or problems that we would not otherwise have noticed.

The potential advantages in extending the range of legal research to include data from foreign legal systems are evident. But the very magnitude of the task entails risks and difficulties. Comparability is always an issue. Even if one focusses on countries at similar stages of development, one cannot compare legal rules, institutions or systems without knowing how they actually function, and one cannot know how they function without situating them in their legal, political, economic and cultural context.[4] This inescapably involves interdisciplinary work with other social sciences, drawing the comparatist into history, philosophy, sociology, economics, and political science. Thus, by its very nature, the comparison of legal systems is a collaborative enterprise, one that often depends heavily on empirical work. European jurists realized long ago that such ambitious undertakings require teamwork. American lawyers, however, have been slow to follow suit; they have yet to establish anything on the order of the great European comparative law institutes.

Given the complexity of the undertaking, the added years of study, and the need to learn other languages, an inquisitive person might wonder why a legal scholar would find it worthwhile to engage in comparative legal studies. One of the oldest reasons is a very practical one: the search for *assistance in law-making*. In Plato's last and longest dialogue, the *Laws,* a Cretan charged with the duty of devising a constitution and legal code for a new colony asks for advice from a Spartan and an Athenian. His superiors have told him that if he discovers some laws from elsewhere that are better than Cretan laws, he is not to worry about their being foreign.[5] At the end of the dialogue, after the three men have finished outlining a legal system for the new city, the Athenian reminds his companions that the law-making process must be an ongoing one since laws are always in need of review in the light of new circumstances. He advises, therefore, that the Guardians of the city should send out mature citizens to study the laws elsewhere, and that they should be open to advice from wise persons of either sex wherever they may be found—not only in cities like Sparta that are famed for good laws, but even in ill-ordered cities like Athens.[6]

---

[3]Maitland (1911), p. 488.

[4]See generally Glendon et al. (2014), pp. 27–28; and Sacco (1991).

[5]*The Laws of Plato*, trans. Pangle (1980), p. 88.

[6]Ibid., 353–356.

To aid national lawmakers was one of the aims of the first European comparative law associations. At a time when European countries were confronting novel problems posed by industrialization and urbanization, it was natural to cast a wide net for ideas. The goal was rarely to find models that could simply be copied or transplanted. The idea was that an awareness of how other nations handle similar problems could provide a deeper understanding of the problems, of how various approaches work out in practice, what advantages they might offer, and what risks or indirect consequences they might entail. Since 1965, the English and Scottish Law Commissions have been required by statute "to obtain such information as to the legal systems of other countries as appears to the Commissioners likely to facilitate the performance of any of their functions."[7] Even in the United States, it is standard practice for lawyers to consult the laws of other states when dealing with new issues or with problems their own jurisdictions are not handling very well.

Although comparative legal study often begins in a search for helpful ideas from elsewhere, a more than incidental benefit, often noted by comparatists, is that the search frequently leads to *a deeper understanding of one's own system*. Our own way of doing things seems so natural to us that often it is only comparison with another way that establishes that there is something to be explained. The French historian Fernand Braudel put it well: "Live in England for a year, and you will not learn much about the English. But when you return to France you will see, in the light of your surprise, that which had remained hidden to you because it was so familiar."[8]

While there are many good practical reasons for undertaking comparative legal studies, I believe most comparatists would say that what holds their interest is primarily *the pursuit of knowledge as an end in itself*. In a 1968 lecture, my teacher Max Rheinstein explained what it was about comparative law that had kept him fascinated for nearly 50 years: "I would state *first* the usefulness our insights have in and by themselves. They are answers, mostly tentative ones, to man's insatiable quest for knowing his world. They are as valuable or as useless as the insights obtained in such sciences as comparative religion, comparative linguistics, biology or physics. They satisfy our curiosity."[9]

The pursuit of comparative law, moreover, seems to be especially *conducive to the generation of productive ideas*—those "aha" moments when a researcher gains insights into the connections among law, behavior, and ideas, and glimpses new pathways to explore. When Max Weber delivered his famous lecture on *Science as a Vocation* in 1917, he observed that in order to accomplish anything worthwhile in one's field, one has to have good ideas, and that, regrettably, good ideas "cannot be forced."[10] Indeed, he noted that, "A man may be an excellent worker yet never have a valuable idea of his own."

---

[7]Law Commission Act, 1965, ch. 22, s. 3(1) f.

[8]Braudel (1958), p. 737.

[9]Rheinstein (1968–1969), p. 423.

[10]Weber (1991), p. 129.

It is true that good ideas do not come on demand and that preparation alone cannot make them happen. But it has long been known that that comparative analysis can make the emergence of insights more likely. That observation is at least as old as the Roman poet Lucretius who wrote: "One thing will grow plain when compared to another; and blind night shall not obliterate the path for thee, before thou hast scanned the ultimate things of nature; so much will things throw light on things."[11]

Just why comparative studies should be productive of insights is hard to say. But cognitive theory suggests that confrontation or comparison of different spheres of meaning increases their probability. It can open up previously unrecognized avenues of inquiry, and stimulate new thinking by shaking up the categories within which we usually operate. Legal sociologist Gunther Teubner has theorized that the confrontation of separate discourses serves as a "shock" or "perturbation" that sparks fresh and fruitful ideas by unsettling habitual ways of thinking.[12] Similarly, when Arthur Koestler reviewed first-hand accounts of path-breaking discoveries in the natural sciences, he claimed to have found that in most cases the common element leading up to them was what he called "bisociation" between separate "thought-matrices"—an encounter that sets in motion a fertile process of uncovering, selecting, re-shuffling, combining and synthesizing data, ideas, and skills.[13]

This aspect of comparative study is not just a matter of interest to legal scholars. When longtime practicing lawyers are asked what qualities they value in an associate, they often say that a pearl beyond price is the associate who, in addition to possessing all the usual legal skills, is able to regularly come up with problem-solving ideas.

I would thus suggest what will always attract some legal minds to comparative legal studies is one of the most powerful drives known to the human species: the unrestricted desire to know. The Saint-Saëns drawing illustrating the motto of the French *Société de Législation Comparée* ("*Jus Unum; Lex Multiplex: Universa Curiositas*") expresses well what makes the study of foreign and comparative law so fascinating for many of us. As imagined by the artist, *Jus* (with its double meaning of "justice" and "the law") is a sturdy tree that branches out into *Lex Multiplex*: laws in all their variety. *Curiositas* is pictured as a wide-eyed little owl perched amidst the leaves and branches of the tree. The starry skies above the tree signify that curiosity extends far beyond law and justice.

3 What Future for Comparative Law?

What might be the role of comparative law in today's increasingly interdependent yet conflict-ridden world? As noted at the outset of these reflections, two powerful and opposing trends are transforming the legal, political, and cultural landscape. On

---

[11]Lucretius, De Rerum Nature, I. lines 1115–1118, translation by Santayana (1910), p. 28.

[12]Teubner (1992), pp. 1453–1456.

[13]Koestler (1964), pp. 108–109, 120.

the one hand, there is a universalizing impulse that has strong appeal in many quarters, especially for international businesspersons, public international lawyers, international civil servants, and human rights activists. On the other, there is an impulse toward decentralization that finds expression in various movements for regional, national and local autonomy and that has strong appeal for persons who are concerned about preserving cultural identity or who seek to have more of a voice in setting the conditions under which they live, work, and raise their children. One force pushes toward unification and standardization; the other toward pluralism and diversity. Both have adherents animated by visions of the good; both have adherents with less lofty motives. There are enormous struggles over whether and how some regional, national, or local legal arrangements should be modified, and over the extent to which those arrangements and the values they represent should be protected.

Legal education has done well in preparing future lawyers to adapt to some aspects of the powerful forces of globalization that are transforming the world. But it has been less attentive to the homogenizing, disrupting thrust of global economic and cultural trends on the diverse cultures and traditions that continue to give most of the world's inhabitants their sense of meaning and identity. And it has been less attentive to the advantages of diversity as a source of creativity and new ideas.

It thus seems appropriate to point out that comparatists could provide a much-needed service to legal education at the present moment. Comparatists are, after all, connoisseurs of cultural difference, probers of particularity, and lovers of local knowledge. For comparatists, legal diversity is not a barrier or a nuisance, but an invitation and an opportunity for exploration.[14] Those inclinations do not make them cultural relativists; rather, they prompt the comparatist to strive mightily to keep the particular in touch with the universal and the universal in touch with the particular; and to show that the ideal of *Jus Unum* can co-exist with *Lex Multiplex.*

That was the aim of the principal framers of the U.N.'s 1948 Universal Declaration of Human Rights. They did not accept the view that recognition of universal rights was irreconcilable with respect for particular cultures. Nor did they believe that acceptance of universal principles could, or should, lead to completely uniform means of expressing and protecting basic rights. They took for granted that there would always be different cultural expressions of the universal human longing for freedom, and different ways of pondering the eternal tensions between freedom and order, the individual and the group. Theirs was a vision of legitimate pluralism in which each country's rights tradition would be enriched as it put the UDHR's general principles into practice, and the various experiences of the nations would in turn enrich the understanding of universal rights.[15]

As Paolo Carozza has pointed out, comparative law "has the paradoxical capacity to deepen our understanding and appreciation of the particularities of legal traditions

---

[14]See Grosswald Curran (1998).

[15]See Glendon (2001), pp. 230–231.

while at the same time helping us to transcend our differences by relating them to one another."[16] Carozza, who combines expertise in the law of continental European nations with public international law and human rights law, has called attention to the need to develop an integrated approach that "values the freedom and integrity of local cultures without reducing particularism to pure devolution..., and [that] affirms internationalism...without the temptation for a super-state or other centralized global authority."[17]

It must be noted, however, that there are reasons for caution concerning the wish often expressed by comparatists that lawyers and policy makers would show more interest in foreign law. As Maitland warned long ago, "there is not much 'comparative jurisprudence' for those who do not know thoroughly well the things to be compared."[18] Then, too, there is the problem of selectivity. As Jean Carbonnier once pointed out, "the invocation of comparative law by a government, or by its opposition, is often only an instrument of propaganda."[19] Both risks are illustrated by the references to foreign law by some U.S. Supreme Court Justices. So far, the Justices who are most enthusiastic for "learning" from other countries have shown little interest in learning from courts that take a different view from theirs on such matters as the admissibility of illegally obtained evidence, the regulation of abortion, the regulation of speech, or public funding for religious education.[20] (Critics have compared their occasional reliance on foreign law to a person who goes to a party and looks over the heads of the crowd, picking out his friends.)[21]

Nevertheless, I would like to think that legal education can help to diminish the misuses of comparative law, and that the future of international legal studies will be marked by fruitful collaboration and interaction among comparatists, public international lawyers, international business law specialists, and all who labor on behalf of human rights.

To that end, and in response to Academy President Katharina Boele-Woelki's request for suggested topics that the Academy might discuss in coming years, I would propose the following for consideration:

1. An exploration of the role of comparative law in the interplay between universalizing, homogenizing trends on the one hand and impulses toward decentralization on the other.
2. A revisitation of the issues examined in the 1992 conference of the International Association of Comparative Law titled "Individualism and Communitarianism in Contemporary Legal Systems: Tensions and Accommodations."[22] Much has

---

[16]Carozza (1997–1998), p. 1236.

[17]Carozza (2003), p. 78.

[18]Maitland (1911).

[19]Carbonnier (1979), p. 201.

[20]Glendon (2014), pp. 17–18.

[21]Roper v. Simmons, 543 U.S. 551, 617 (2005), (Scalia, J., dissenting).

[22]The General Report and National Reports were published in 1993 Brigham Young University Law Review, Issue No. 2.

changed since that conference was held, especially concerning the balance between individualism and communitarianism in each legal system's treatment of the family, the world of work, schools, and the various intermediate institutions of civil society.
3. An exploration of the meaning of subsidiarity in national and international law.

References

Braudel F (1958) Histoire et Sciences Sociales: La longue durée. In: Annales: Economies, sociétés, civilisations, pp 725–753
Carbonnier J (1979) A beau mentir qui vient du loin. Essais sur les lois (Répertoire du Notariat Defrénois)
Carozza P (1997–1998) Uses and misuses of comparative law in international human rights: some reflections on the jurisprudence of the European Court of Human Rights. Notre Dame Law Rev 73:1217
Carozza P (2003) Subsidiarity as a structural principle of international human rights law. Am J Int Law 97:38
Durkheim E (1966) The rules of sociological method. Free Press, New York
Glendon MA (2001) A world made new: Eleanor Roosevelt and the universal declaration of human rights. Random House
Glendon MA (2014) Comparative law in the age of globalization. Duquesne Law Rev 52:1
Glendon MA, Carozza PG, Picker CB (2014) Comparative legal traditions, 4th edn. West
Grosswald Curran V (1998) Cultural immersion, difference and categories in U.S. comparative law. Am J Comp Law 46:43
Koestler A (1964) The act of creation: a study of the conscious and unconscious processes of humor, scientific discovery, and art. Macmillan, New York
Maitland FW (1911) Why the history of English Law is not written. In: Collected Papers of Frederic William Maitland, vol I. Cambridge University Press
Pangle TL (1980) The Laws of Plato, translated with notes and an interpretive essay. Basic Books, New York
Rheinstein M (1968–69) Comparative law: its functions, methods, and usages. Arkansas Law Rev 22:415
Sacco R (1991) Legal formants: a dynamic approach to comparative law (I and II). Am J Comp Law 39:1 and 343
Santayana G (1910) Three philosophical poets: Lucretius, Dante, Goethe. Harvard University Press
Teubner G (1992) The two faces of Janus: rethinking legal pluralism. Cardozo Law Rev 13:1443
Weber M (1991) Science as a vocation. In: Gerth H, Wright Mills C (eds) From max weber: essays in sociology. Routledge, London, pp 129–156
Zweigert K, Kötz HD (1998) An introduction to comparative law, 3rd edn. Oxford University Press

The Quiet Persuader Between the Forum and the Tower

Marta Cartabia

1 Introduction

It is great honor and joy to celebrate Mary Ann Glendon's outstanding contribution to comparative legal studies. Indeed, she is one of the most prominent comparative legal scholars. It suffices here to recall *Comparative legal traditions*,[1] a successful textbook, written with Paolo Carozza and Colin Pickel, published in four editions, an evergreen in its approach to comparative law. However, to me, Mary Ann Glendon is even much more than that. She is not only a distinguished comparatist, and even a pioneer of this branch of academic study. She is a public intellectual. And—even more relevantly—she is an inspiring woman.

I would say that her scholarship is so charming, rich, creative, vivid, pathbreaking, visionary, and thought-provoking because she is more than a mere academic; in my eyes—and in the eyes of many—she is an outstanding intellectual who draws inspiration and energy from her commitments both in her personal life and in the public square. The richness of her life is reflected in the unique style of her scholarship, which combines sensitivity, elegance, freshness, clear sight, originality, courage, openness, and balance.

She belongs to that family of jurists who are complete, learned humanists rather than mere trained, technical professionals. Her legal reasoning is based on culture, experience, and practical reason, as opposed to mere logic and deductive reasoning. For Mary Ann Glendon, "The life of the law has not been [pure] logic: it has been

[1]Glendon et al. (2014).

M. Cartabia (✉)
Italian Constitutional Court, Milan, Italy
e-mail: marta.cartabia@cartabia.eu

K. Boele-Woelki, D. P. Fernàndez Arroyo (eds.), *The Past, Present and Future of Comparative Law - Le passé, le présent et le futur du droit comparé*, Ius Comparatum – Global Studies in Comparative Law 29, https://doi.org/10.1007/978-3-319-93770-0_2

experience" as Justice Oliver Wendell Holmes would put it. As she herself attests,[2] her work has been built on the methodological approach of her mentor in Chicago—Max Rheinstein—a distinguished scholar of comparative law and student of Max Weber. He left a mark on her scholarship, since she learnt from him how to employ both sociological and legal methods to explore the interaction among law, behavior, and ideas; and law, culture, history and society.

2 Tradition at the Center

Given this background, it should come as no surprise that at the center of her comparative work is the idea of "tradition". When she compares different legal systems, she does not merely consider simple pieces of legislation or a bunch of written texts having legally binding force. While she does, indeed, take into due account all the "legal formants"—as Professor Rodolfo Sacco would say[3]—including legislation, cases and scholarly interpretations, she goes further than that. She broadens the focus of her investigation so as to embrace the social, historical, and cultural dimensions of law. In her view, law is part of a "living tradition", in Alasdair MacIntyre's sense of "an historically extended" and "socially embodied"[4] narrative, whose developments constantly point beyond itself.[5] Or, in John Merryman's definition, "a set of deeply rooted, historically conditioned attitudes about the nature of law, about the role of law in the society and the polity, about the proper organization and operation of a legal system, and about the way law is or should be made, applied, studied, perfected and taught".[6]

In a way, her idea of law as legal tradition echoes Haberle's theory of (constitutional) law as culture[7] or Santi Romano's theory of law as a social institution.[8]

Generally speaking, the idea of "tradition" is considered to be a part of the vocabulary of the conservative culture. However, in Mary Glendon's thought tradition has an original meaning. It is not opposed to change, innovation, and progress—which usually belong to the vocabulary of the progressive culture. In her view, tradition is not the reductive idea against which modernity has revolted. It is not a conservative notion, a chilling or freezing concept; it is not the dead hand of the past, made of old prejudices and power relations; it is not antithetical to creativity, nor is it static.

---

[2]Yearbook 2010, The Pontifical Academy of Sciences, Vatican City 2010, 31.

[3]Sacco (1991).

[4]MacIntyre (1981), p. 207.

[5]Glendon (2006), p. 4.

[6]Merryman and Pérez-Perdomo (2007), p. 2.

[7]Häberle (1998).

[8]Romano (1946).

"In the minds of many people, the word 'tradition' evokes a vision of the frozen and static past. As we use it here, however, it denotes a vital, dynamic, ongoing system".[9]

Law as tradition designates, for her, a body of norms, a being that lives and grows, that preserves its identity while every atom of which it is composed is subject to a ceaseless process of change, decay, and renewal.

Adaptation, growing, continuity, and ongoing self-correction are the main features of tradition. Consequently, tradition is not opposed to reason, and continuity is not incompatible with innovation. In fact, one of the Mary Ann Glendon's favorite quotes is Justice Cardozo's aphorism that, "in the endless process of testing and retesting, there is a constant rejection of the dross".[10]

"Living law"—as the Austrian sociologist of law Eugene Ehlrich puts it—is probably a good proxy for Glendon's idea of tradition; an adequate notion to approach the legal reality of a community.

Community: indeed, the communitarian element is implied in the idea of tradition. Tradition is the work of a community, not of a single individual, however ingenious that person might be: being rooted in a living tradition means being a part of an extended process of collaboration over time; it is a group achievement, defined and refined over centuries by generations of men and women.

In a word, tradition in Mary Ann Glendon's scholarship has a double essential feature: it is dynamic and it is communitarian.

3 Glendon's Moral Realism: Family, Property, Welfare, Legal Profession and Rights Talk

Glendon's early comparative analysis focuses on some crucial legal aspects where transformations in traditional institutions were (and still are) highly dramatic. Her earliest works in the 1970s traced the relationship between changes in property law and changes in the family's role as a determinant of economic security and social standing in modern societies.[11] She also turned to comparative labor law and welfare legislation, the legal profession,[12] abortion and divorce,[13] and individual rights.[14]

Concerned with the morality of law, she avoids moralism in her statements about the failure of law. As Donald P. Kommers[15] puts it, Glendon's approach can be characterized as moral realism, an approach that pays close attention to cultural

[9]Glendon et al. (2014), p. 34.

[10]Cardozo (1921), p. 179.

[11]Glendon (1977, 1989a).

[12]Glendon (1996).

[13]Glendon (1989b).

[14]Glendon (1991).

[15]Kommers (1998), p. 1334.

differences and to the evolving social reality in her critical appraisal of American law and does not overstate the role of law in the moral wellbeing of a given society. She views with dismay the breakdown of family ties, under pressure from an individualistic culture that is spreading in the American social and legal environment; she considers the family to be a relevant institution, a "seedbed of civic virtue", and an important mediating structure between the individual and the State to be preserved for the sake of human flourishing and for the common good. Nonetheless, she doubts the law's capacity to substantially change or redirect the march of social and cultural events, which are heavily resistant to law's influence.

Her interests in the major transformations of social life brought her to reconsider the evolution of individual rights in American society in her masterpiece *Rights Talk*. Glendon first explored the realm of individual civil rights in practice, with her personal commitment as a young lawyer in the Sixties. Thirty years later she revisits the matter from a theoretical point of view and notices a dramatic change in American law: she uncovers the ambivalence of the idea of rights and its possible drawbacks.

In her passionate and powerful criticism of the libertarian/individualistic dialect of human rights which invaded America in the latter half of the Twentieth century, Mary Ann Glendon[16] has convincingly shown how the insistence on privacy and individual liberty cultivates a society of lonely people, waters down all sense of responsibility, and disrupts all sorts of social ties that at the time of the foundation of the United States were taken for granted in social life. All the relational dimensions of the human person are disregarded and dispersed, and, with them, all idea of being responsible not only for one's own individual success, but also for the common good.

Yet hers is not an utter critique of individual rights. Her critical analysis does not turn into a sheer dismissal of the concept. She rather attacks the absoluteness of individualism in recent "American rights dialect":

> Absoluteness is an illusion and hardly a harmless one. When we assert our rights to life, liberty and property, we are expressing the reasonable hope that such things can be made more secure by law and politics. When we assert these rights in an absolute form, however, we are expressing infinite and impossible desires – to be completely free, to possess things totally, to be captain of our fate, and masters of our souls. There is a pathos as well as a bravado in these attempts to deny the fragility and the contingency of human existence, personal freedom, and the possession of worldly goods [...] Thus, for example, those who contest the legitimacy of mandatory automobile seat-belt or motorcycle helmet law frequently say: 'It's my body and I have the rights to do as I please with it'. However, the paradox of human existence is that 'the independent individualistic, helmetless and free on the open road, becomes the most dependent of individuals in the spinal injury ward.'[17]

A twenty-first-century reader of Mary Ann Glendon's comparative work on individual rights would probably notice an optimistic analysis of the European tradition as compared to the American one. To put it differently: in her work on

[16]See Glendon (1991), pp. 47–144.

[17]Glendon (1991), pp. 45–46.

Rights Talk, she stresses the difference between the American libertarian and individualistic dialect and the European one, which she qualifies as dignitarian. The former implies and promotes an impoverished image of the human person, a "lone rights-bearer", an atomistic individual with little or no connection to family, place, church, workplace, or community. The latter, while preserving an elevated status for individual rights, employs a richer lexicon, encompassing the language of responsibility and sociality. In this respect, she underscores the difference between American and European legal traditions.

As a European legal scholar and judge of the twenty-first century, I would say that the divide between the individualistic-libertarian and the personalistic-dignitarian brands of rights is less geographical than chronological in nature. The move towards an individualistic understanding of human rights first took place on the American side of the Atlantic and some 25 years later reached European shores. Now the two sides of western rights culture are converging towards a more individualistic social—and consequently—legal life. The question arises: had her masterpiece on *Rights Talk* been written today, would it still emphasize the difference between the two western rights dialects?

At present, the critics of individual rights are becoming more vocal in the European context as well.[18] They tend to restore the language of duties and responsibilities that was downplayed in the last decades because of the pervasiveness of rights talk. In this context, more aware of the social depression and fragmentation produced by the excess of the libertarian-individualistic legal culture, the contribution of Mary Glendon could usefully circulate in the European theatre as an illuminating account of the limits of such a precious achievement of western constitutionalism as individual rights have been and still are.

4 A Restless Builder of Social Ties

In her critical appraisal of the libertarian rights dialect, Mary Ann shows a level of moral concern, but she cannot be characterized as a public moralist. Despite her clear and public identity as a catholic legal thinker, in her books she is never one-sided, nor is she apologetic. She is such a sympathetic and passionate advocate of all human attempts to be a natural supporter of pluralism and diversity.

As it has been said, "Glendon's work bears the imprint of her personal biography."[19] For her, crossing cultural lines and embracing diversity, is not only a matter of intellectual speculation; it is first and foremost a matter of personal experience. Her family has always been a daily celebration of diversity: a multi-cultural, multi-ethnic, and multi-religious environment, and—to borrow one of her central ideas—a

[18] Just in Italy, only as examples, see at least: Violante (2017) and Zagrebelsky (2017).

[19] Kommers (1998), p. 1352.

veritable "seedbed of virtue" or, if you will, a "school of citizenship", where tolerance, respect, and group discussion are practiced and cultivated.

She has also practiced the virtue of the restless builder of social ties in her service in the public square of her country, which began as early as the 1960s, when she worked as a volunteer lawyer in the civil rights movement in Mississippi. Her route in the public forum has had more recent relevant milestones in her appointment at the US President's Council of Bioethics (2000–2004), as US Ambassador to the Holy See (2008–2009), and as a member of the US Commission on International Religious Freedom (USCIRF) (2012–2016).

No less relevant has been her remarkable diplomatic experience involving the Roman Catholic Church, which she began by holding the leading position in the Vatican delegation to the international 1995 Beijing Conference on Women, sponsored by the United Nations; she then served as President of the Pontifical Academy of Social Sciences (1994–2014), later as a member (2013–2014) of the Pontifical Commission of Inquiry for the Institute for Works of Religion (IOR), and, since 2014, as a member of the board of the Vatican Bank (IOR). Her involvement with the Catholic Church has been—among other things—an opportunity to engage in a very diverse and pluralistic community of more than one billion people on all corners of the globe.

Last, but not least, the research and teaching she has carried out, first at Boston College, and then at the prestigious Harvard Law School, since 1986, are anything but parochial or repetitive: they encompass family and property law, constitutional law, international human rights, political philosophy and, indeed, comparative legal traditions. She herself likes to repeat that her "adventure" as a scholar of comparative law is nicely expressed by the motto of the French Société de la Législation Comparée: *Jus unum, lex multiplex, universa curiositas.*[20] I think that this phrase really says so much about her intellectual curiosity, open-mindedness, and warm personality.

5 Mary Ann and Eleanor

Interestingly enough, Glendon's professional trajectory is mirrored in her most recent book—*The forum and the tower*[21]—a collection of the biographies of some twelve scholars who have accepted to spend a good part of their professional energy as statespersons, ranging from Plato to Eleanor Roosevelt. Mary Ann Glendon herself could have been included in one of the chapters of the book: it stresses the

[20]This concept was expressed in a very personal speech that Mary Ann Glendon gave in a workshop for the celebration of her 75th anniversary in Florence, that I had the pleasure to convene at together with my friends and colleagues Paolo Carozza and Andrea Simoncini, with whom I share the privilege of a special friendship with Professor Glendon.

[21]Glendon (2011).

importance that statespersons keep in touch with the world of ideas and that political and legal theorists should attend to what is going on in the life of the polity. It also reflects on the different virtues required of public figures and of intellectuals in their respective sphere of life:

> As a professor, I was responsible primarily for coming up with the best answer I could divine. As policymaker, I was also responsible for the worst that could happen,

reads a phrase by Henry Kissinger that is quoted in the Preface.[22]

The book shows that the qualities that make an excellent scholar or teacher do not always coincide with the qualities that make and effective public actor. Yet, unlike many of the towering figures described in the book, Mary Ann Glendon has both sets of qualities: idealism and realism go hand in hand in her scholarship and in her contribution to public life. Every word and every action of hers speak of a positive realism, of a constructive, optimistic pragmatism. In an article that appeared on The New York Times on the occasion of the United Nations Conference on Women in Beijing in 1995, Fox Butterfield reported what some of her colleagues said about her:

> "Ms. Glendon [is] an insightful and probing scholar [who is] charming and persuasive and can be authoritative without being overbearing".[23] "If you think of a person who you would want to bring two sides together to see where there is a common ground, it is her".[24] Behind her charm, Ms. Glendon can be relentlessly tenacious on the principles she holds dear.[25]

For all these reasons, the book that most represents her in my mind is *A World Made New*,[26] in which she tells the story of Eleanor Roosevelt and the negotiation of the Universal Declaration of Human Rights.

The book speaks of human rights: this echoes her deep commitment to civil rights and the search for shared moral values, the roots necessary for the flourishing of human family and social life, although she sees the limits of human rights project.

It also recounts challenging negotiations: the protagonist is tirelessly engaged in healing divergences and cultural cleavages in the midst of a number of defying crises: the Cold War, the Palestine crisis, the conflicts in China and Korea, and the Berlin blockade, among many others. It shows Mrs. Roosevelt exceptional diplomatic skills, feminine charm, endurance, and patience, in front of a task that was close to a "mission impossible." Like the protagonist of the book, Mary Glendon is a "quiet persuader",[27] a successful, smart, and patient diplomat.

Moreover, the book shows comparative legal traditions in action: in the Human Rights Commission chaired by Mrs. Roosevelt, all the major cultural traditions were represented, and they were looking for common ground and convergences on

[22]Glendon (2011), p. 2.

[23]Laurence H. Tribe, Professor of Constitutional Law at Harvard.

[24]D. Blankenhorn, founder and president of the Institute for American Values.

[25]Butterfield (1995), in the occasion of her nomination as the head of the Vatican delegation in Beijing.

[26]Glendon (2002).

[27]Butterfield (1995).

fundamental values, in the name of human dignity. When the divisions and disagreements became serious, almost insurmountable—not only between the Soviet bloc representatives and the members from the West, but between the more philosophically-inclined and the more practical-minded members—Mrs. Roosevelt invited a number of them for a tea at her Washington Square apartment, persuaded as she was of the benefits of enabling people to get to know one another at a personal level, in an informal atmosphere.

Who is this host persuaded of the benefits of personal relations even in the face of the toughest political undertaking? Here the figure of Mrs. Roosevelt and the smiling visage of Professor Glendon overlap in my mind.

A *World Made New* tells a story of success. The Universal Declaration was approved with a large consensus, and it later brought forth countless pacts, bodies, covenants, and conventions, and a commission for the protection of human rights all around the world.

And yet, in this story there is no space for triumphalism: the narrative is imbued with a great dose of realism, and the conclusion is even more cautious. As Jacques Maritain commented at the end of the enterprise: "whether the music played on the Declaration's thirty strings will be 'in tune with, or harmful to, human dignity', will depend primarily on the extent to which a 'culture of human dignity' develops."[28]

Like the Universal Declaration of Human Rights, every undertaking in the public sphere is unfinished business. But, as Mary Ann Glendon—echoing Bob Dylan—would say: "You have to 'keep on keepin' on".[29] And Mary Ann never gives up: she keeps on keeping on.

References

Butterfield F (1995) U.N. women's forum is a test for Pope's advocate. New York Times of 29 August 1995

Cardozo BN (1921) The nature of the judicial process. Yale University Press, New Haven

Carozza P, Cartabia M (eds) (2007) Tradizioni in subbuglio. Rubbettino, Soveria Mannelli

Glendon MA (1977) State, law and family: family law in transition in the United States and Western Europe. North-Holland Publishing Co., Amsterdam

Glendon MA (1989a) The transformation of family law. State, law, and family in the United States and Western Europe. The University of Chicago Press, Chicago

Glendon MA (1989b) Abortion and divorce in western law. Harvard University Press, Cambridge (MA)

Glendon MA (1991) Rights talk: the impoverishment of political discourse. The Free Press, New York

Glendon MA (1996) A nation under lawyers. Harvard University Press, Cambridge (MA)

Glendon MA (2002) A world made new: Eleanor Roosevelt and the Universal Declaration of Human Rights. Random House, New York

[28]Maritain (1949), pp. 9, 16 quoted in Glendon (2006), p. 347. The Italian translation, *Tradizioni in subbuglio*, is edited by Carozza and Cartabia (2007), p. 73.

[29]Bob Dylan, Tangled Up in Blue.

Glendon MA (2006) Traditions in turmoil. Sapientia Press of Ave Maria University, Ann Arbor
Glendon MA (2011) The forum and the tower: how scholars and politicians have imagined the world, from Plato to Eleanor Roosevelt. Oxford University Press, Oxford
Glendon MA, Carozza PG, Picker CB (2014) Comparative legal traditions. Text, materials and cases on western law, 4th edn. West Publising Co., St Paul
Häberle P (1998) Verfassungslehre als Kulturwissenschaft. Schriften zum Öffentlichen Recht. Duncker & Humblot, Berlin
Kommers DP (1998) The constitutionalism of Mary Ann Glendon. Notre Dame Law Rev 73:1153
Macintyre A (1981) After virtue. A study in moral theory. University of Notre Dame Press, Notre Dame
Maritain J (1949) Introduction. In: UNESCO (ed) Human rights: comments and interpretations. Wingate, London & New York
Merryman J, Pérez-Perdomo R (2007) The civil law tradition: an introduction to the legal systems of Europe and Latin America, 3rd edn. Stanford University Press, Stanford
Romano S (1946) L'ordinamento giuridico. Sansoni, Firenze
Sacco R (1991) Legal formants: a dynamic approach to comparative law (Installment I of II). Am J Comp Law 39:1–34 and 343–401
Violante L (2017) Il dovere di avere doveri. Einaudi, Torino
Zagrebelsky G (2017) Diritti per forza. Einaudi, Torino

Remerciements/Acknowledgements

Mary Ann Glendon

Thank you so much, dear Justice Cartabia, for your exceedingly generous words. It is a very special honor to be presented by a person who is not only a renowned comparatist, but also the Vice-President of one of the world's most respected constitutional courts. And what an honor to find myself here in the company of four great jurists from all of whom I have learned so much over the years!

Madame la Présidente de l'Académie : Quand je pense au fait que cette Académie a compté parmi ses membres tant de grands comparatistes du passé, des véritables géants auxquels nous tous sommes redevables, je suis vraiment profondément touchée.

C'est pourquoi, à cette heureuse occasion, je voudrais évoquer la mémoire d'un de ces maîtres–celui qui m'a introduit au droit comparé: Max Rheinstein, qui est bien connu aussi de à mes quatre collègues. Pour moi, l'esprit ouvert de Rheinstein, sa soif de savoir, et sa curiosité envers le monde ont toujours représenté ce qu'il y a de mieux dans la poursuite du droit comparé.

Ces qualités sont parfaitement illustrées dans l'emblème de la Société Française pour la Législation Comparée (dont Justice Cartabia a déjà fait mention): *Jus Unum, Lex Multiplex, Universa Curiositas*. Etudier le droit comparé, c'est faire l'expérience d'être touché par le désir illimité de savoir; c'est connaître un peu la passion qui brûlait si fort chez Pascal que, selon Tocqueville, Pascal « mourut de vieillesse avant d'avoir quarante ans ».

Madame la Présidente, je voudrais aussi exprimer mon appréciation pour le rôle que l'Académie a joué dans la promotion de l'étude du droit comparé. À notre époque, où le droit a été si profondément affecté par la mondialisation, il me semble que les

M. A. Glendon (✉)
Harvard University, Cambridge, MA, USA
e-mail: glendon@law.harvard.edu

K. Boele-Woelki, D. P. Fernàndez Arroyo (eds.), *The Past, Present and Future of Comparative Law - Le passé, le présent et le futur du droit comparé*, Ius Comparatum – Global Studies in Comparative Law 29, https://doi.org/10.1007/978-3-319-93770-0_3

comparatistes ont des contributions essentielles à apporter. Avec leurs compétences dans la médiation entre l'universel et le particulier, ils savent apprécier l'intégrité des cultures locales sans réduire le particularisme à la décentralisation pure. En même temps, ils savent apprécier l'internationalisme sans être trop attirés par les idées de l'autorité hyper-centralisée.

Enfin, Madame la Présidente, dans la réjouissance à l'avance de nos discussions sur le passé, le présent et l'avenir du droit comparé, j'aimerais vous remercier très sincèrement pour cet honneur.

Partie II / Part II
Hein D. Kötz

Comparative Law: A Veteran's View

Hein D. Kötz

The International Academy of Comparative Law invited five veterans of the field to state their views on "The Past, the Present and the Future of Comparative Law". Their task was made easier by various questions asked by the President of the Academy, Ms. *K. Boele-Woelki*. The following text is an extended and supplemented version of my answers.[1]

1. One question the President of the Academy suggested we should answer was related to the *method of comparative law*. It is indeed true that over the last 20 years many critical questions have been asked on that subject. I published a book on comparative law in 1998 which is, I believe, widely regarded as the "classical" restatement of methodological orthodoxy[2] and has on that ground been attacked as being outdated, *démodé*, antiquated and out of touch with the challenges comparative law is facing today. Let me describe in a little more detail the grounds on which the "classical" approach has been criticized.

One kind of criticism remains on a fairly conventional level. It has been said, for example, that one of the shortcomings of current mainstream comparative law is its emphasis on *private law*.[3] There is indeed no doubt that comparative law scholars not only in Europe but also in the United States have overwhelmingly been private law scholars. They have demonstrated the use of comparative law by making reference to the law of contract, tort and property, to family law and the law of

[1] A few footnotes were added, but I made no attempt to convert my answers into a learned article.

[2] Zweigert and Kötz (1998) and Zimmermann (2006), p. 551.

[3] See, for example, Reimann (1998), p. 639 f.

H. D. Kötz (✉)
Max Planck Institute for Comparative and International Private Law, Hamburg, Germany
e-mail: koetz@mpipriv.de

K. Boele-Woelki, D. P. Fernàndez Arroyo (eds.), *The Past, Present and Future of Comparative Law - Le passé, le présent et le futur du droit comparé*, Ius Comparatum – Global Studies in Comparative Law 29, https://doi.org/10.1007/978-3-319-93770-0_4

succession. It is also true that the available teaching materials focus entirely on traditional private law topics. The argument is that while this focus may have been appropriate in the last century it should no longer enjoy dominant status in the current world. Today constitutional questions, administrative procedures, regulatory regimes and criminal law and procedure have become highly significant and may well overshadow the importance of private entitlements. Another criticism is based on the view that mainstream comparative law, particularly in the European context, is mainly concerned with "*black letter rules*" with little or no attention to the "law in action", to the practice of the courts, to arbitration, to the institutional and procedural context, to rulemaking by private institutions, and indeed to the predispositions, mentalities, or habits of legal cultures.[4] *Lawrence Friedman* has argued that what matters is not what black letter rules say but "the extent to which they are embedded in societies with similar social structures, institutions and social codes."[5]

A further more radical step has been taken by critics who view mainstream comparative law as a totally sterile, barren and fruitless undertaking. Some of them seem to start at what may be called a post-modernist platform. They argue that "classical" comparative law is based on the erroneous and fallacious idea that legal rules can be "compared" at all and that they may on that ground be considered as "similar", as "convergent", or as "performing the same function". What should be stressed instead is the complexity and ambiguity of legal systems and the extent to which they are based on unbridgeable differences of legal culture and mentalities. Authors of this school favour legal pluralism, wonder whether language and cultural barriers can really be overcome, and take a dim view of the possibility of harmonizing or assimilating legal rules. *Pierre Legrand* has taken the position that different legal cultures are ultimately incommensurate, that it is impossible for a French lawyer to really understand what an English judge is saying, and that the idea of "convergence", if applied to legal systems, is a pipedream and a chimera.[6]

These critics have certainly raised a number of important points. However, I do not think, that the death-knell has been sounded to "classical" comparative law. Nor do I think that there are reasons why comparative lawyers of the more traditionalist school must now throw up their hands in despair. What the critics I refer to have in common is their view that the basic mistake of "classical" comparative law is its

---

[4]See for example, Reimann (2002), p. 693.

[5]Friedman (1990), p. 54.

[6]See below n. 21 and accompanying text. See also Michaels (2012), p. 298: He distinguishes two fundamentally different methods of comparative law. One is based on the principle of "functionalism" and is therefore called "functional comparison". The other method is described as "cultural comparison". Its focus "lies on the mentality expressed in a legal system, which is not fully observable by outsiders and can only be experienced by those raised, and operating, within this respective system. Because cultural differences (particularly those between civil law and common law) are seen as unbridgeable and because different legal cultures are deemed worthy of protection, cultural comparison usually opposes comparative evaluation and legal unification as both impossible and undesirable. Instead, it promotes tolerance for foreign law and for difference in general."

reliance on the principle of "functionality". However, the discrepancies between "functional" and "cultural" comparison are much "smaller than the sometimes fierce debate suggests".[7] The principle of "functionality" means that in law the only things which are comparable are those which fulfill the same function. Solutions in different jurisdictions must therefore be cut loose from their conceptual context and stripped of their national doctrinal structures. They become comparable only when it has been shown that they serve the same function and satisfy the same need. In determining the functional equivalence comparative lawyers must avoid all limitations and restraints. They must take into account whatever moulds or affects or influences human conduct, be it statute law, case law, customary law, legal writings, standard-form contracts, trade usages, the availability of informal techniques of dispute resolution etc. In some cases one may come to the conclusion that a certain problem is solved in different jurisdictions by quite different technical means though with the same practical result. In these cases one may say that the "presumption of similarity" applies.[8] However, the opposite conclusion may be reached in other cases, and it is clearly compatible with the "functional" approach to comparative law to search for the reasons—including "cultural reasons"—that may explain the differences between the different solutions of different jurisdictions. Let me give you a few examples.

Take the case of products liability in the United States and Europe. The conditions of liability are equally strict in both jurisdictions. However, substantial differences appear once you take into account—as you must—the general institutional context in which the law of products liability has evolved and is actually applied in the United States and in Europe. You will then have to discuss the role of the American jury, the allocation of litigation expenses, contingent fees, punitive damages, the robust discovery tools available to the plaintiff's lawyer even at the expense of the defendant's business or personal privacy, and the fact that it is not only possible, but quite common for many thousands of similar claims to be bundled together and dealt with in the single trial of a class action. In other words: Product liability litigation in the United States is very different from what we have in this field in Europe. But this is not where the comparative endeavour should stop. The comparative lawyer must cast his net wider still. He might say, for example, that while all developed legal systems must ensure the safety of products in the interest of the consumer the Americans, with their deep-seated mistrust of governmental authority and impartiality, do not rely—as we do in Europe—on the initiative of administrators or public prosecutors, but rather on private litigation as the chief regulator of corporate action in the product liability field. It is true that this idea has

---

[7] Michaels (2012), p. 299.

[8] Although the "*praesumtio similitudinis*" was first introduced in all innocence by Zweigert and Kötz (1998), p. 40, it has meanwhile become the favourite scapegoat, whipping boy and arch-enemy of the *aficionados* of what is called the "cultura" approach to comparative law. What the critics tend to overlook is that the "functional" approach has no difficulties whatsoever in accepting the diagnosis of deep-seated *differences* between the solutions of different jurisdictions. See, for example Dannemann (2006), p. 383.

nothing to do with the technicalities of product liability. It may be at home in political science, welfare economics or sociology or in what may be called "American legal culture". I do not really care. What I do care for is that comparative lawyers reveal *all* factors regardless of their origin or provenance that shed light in some way or other on the reasons explaining the similarities and differences of the solutions accepted in different jurisdictions.

Let me give you another example. If you look at modern Chinese statute law dealing with a contracting party's liability for damages in the event of a breach of contract you will probably not be surprised to see that there are no major differences between the Chinese law in the books and the rules we are used to in the civil law and the common law. However, there is evidence showing that Chinese statute law has in this field little practical significance, perhaps because going to court is considered to be rude, ill-mannered or ungentlemanly, or because court actions take too long, judges are not impartial, and the execution of court orders against obstinant parties is unheard of. If actions for damages for breach of contract are rare or non-existent in China what other sanctions are there to explain why sellers, building contractors and other contracting parties tend to live up to their contractual promises? How do you explain the tremendous rates of growth in the Chinese economy in the absence of effective legal remedies? One explanation is that what parties in breach of their contractual stipulations really fear in contemporary China are not court actions, but administrative sanctions taken by the state bureaucracy and the Communist party standing behind it. This may include the revocation of governmental permits, the investigation of suspected violations or the imposition of fines. Statements to this effect have mostly been made by economists,[9] and I do not know whether there is any empirical evidence on which these statements can be based. What I would suggest, however, is that a comparative lawyer worth his salt must take them into account no matter where he finds them and what academic discipline supports them.

The critics of traditional comparative law have also accused it of a failure to become truly interdisciplinary.[10] I agree that performance has been lagging. In the law as elsewhere there is of course the well-known tendency to preach interdisciplinarity while still remaining within the limits of the original discipline. It is true that the autonomy of legal scholarship still finds considerable support even though it is based only on the highly technical and formalized character of the law, the depth of professional pride and the relative isolation of the law professors from their colleagues of the other social science departments. Even so, I think that the law in general and comparative law in particular must be open to the ideas and influences of the other social sciences. In particular, comparative lawyers should not underestimate the explanatory power of economic analysis. Let me illustrate this by a little story. When I was a visiting professor at the University of Chicago Law School nearly 50 years ago *Richard Posner* was busily working on the first edition of his book on the "Economic Analysis of Law" in an office next to mine. When we had

[9]See, for example, Cooter and Schäfer (2012), pp. 37, 90 ff.

[10]Reimann (2002), p. 685.

had some discussions about our mutual fields of interest he came one day into my office picking me up for lunch at the Faculty Club. "Look, Hein", he said, "you keep telling me that different legal systems, despite the enormous differences in their conceptual structures, often produce similar solutions for the same practical problems. What better explanation is there for this phenomenon than that all judges draw their inspiration from the same secret root of economic logic?" Might it not be argued that judges and legislators, like Monsieur Jourdain who did not know he was talking prose, are driven to their conclusions by the same economic logic and that this logic, which is certainly of universal application, will tend to produce the same or similar results?

Let me come back for a moment to the question I asked at the beginning: What would I change if I were to publish a new book about comparative law? I think that a lot would have to be changed or put into a form less amenable to misunderstandings. There is indeed no doubt that statements which seemed to go without saying 20 or 30 years ago arc now widely debated. This is a good thing because, as *Jean de la Fontaine* said in one of his fables, "*la dispute est d'un grand secours; sans elle on dormirait toujours*".[11] On the other hand, it is my conviction that legal theory in general and comparative legal theory in particular are only tools, and that the only standard for judging their worth is the extent to which they help us penetrate to the essentials of real issues of the practical world. It seems to me, however, that many academic attacks on mainstream comparative law see their audience exclusively in other academics and are only intended to circulate within the closed medium of academic discussion with little or no spillover into the world of action.

2. Another question asked by the President of the Academy referred to the role comparative law should take in *legal education*. Now it is common knowledge that no passion exceeds that of a law professor for his favourite course, and if you ask a comparative lawyer about the importance of his field of interest in legal education the answer is clear. Nor is there any doubt about the reasons why comparative law has an important educational value for the teaching of young lawyers. It is nonetheless true that European law schools draw heavily on the law of the country where these schools sit, often banishing comparative law into marginal introductory courses or pushing it off into specialized seminars. True, there are some signs of improvement in recent years. There are the *Erasmus* and *Socrates* programmes, there are special degree programmes for foreign students, and some law schools, in particular in the Netherlands and Bucerius Law School in Hamburg of which Ms *Boele-Woelki* is the current dean, have pioneered the integration of national law and the laws of other European countries. Nonetheless courses are still very rare in which the law of contract, company law or other fields are discussed in depth from a comparative perspective. Should this not become the rule? Should comparative law be integrated into the teaching of national law? Was *Roscoe Pound* right when he said in 1934 that

[11]See his fable on "Le chat et le renard": Livre IX, Fable 14.

> comparative law will best be taught, for the purposes of our professional instruction, in the course of the teaching the law of the land.[12]

Should we not follow in Europe the American example? In the United States "national law schools" do not teach the law of the state where they sit. Instead they teach American law as if it existed, and young lawyers will be admitted to the legal profession on the basis of state bar examinations that examine nearly exclusively on "national general principles of common law" rather than the law of any particular state. I sympathize with such a re-orientation of the curriculum of European law schools. On the other hand, I must admit that this may be overambitious, premature and impracticable at the present stage. If such changes are to come they will only come when the real world creates a demand for them, in other words, when European political and economic integration has reached a stage requiring a different type of legal education and a different type of lawyer. The signs are already on the wall, particularly in the smaller European countries. But I do not think that we have reached that stage on a general basis yet.

3. I would like to conclude with a few words about the role of comparative law in the *Europeanization* of law.[13] In this field comparative legal studies have "indeed gained a momentum and a significance unprecedented in the last hundred years."[14] One major reason is that the harmonization and unification of private law has been one of the main agenda of the European Union. Uniform EU rules have addressed important areas of competition law, company law, labour law and international private law. Some 20 EU directives were passed in an attempt to ensure that the laws of the Member States afford a substantially harmonized minimum level of consumer protection. The EU has asked a Study Group to put the "*Acquis Communautaire*"—in other words: the existing EU law—into a more orderly and systematic form,[15] and it has also encouraged another Study Group to develop a "Common Frame of Reference" intended to serve as a "tool kit" for future harmonization or unification projects. A "Commission on European Contract Law"—a body without any official status based on the initiative of Professor *Ole Lando*—prepared the "Principles of European Contract Law" which constitute today the most advanced and internationally most widely noted restatement of European Contract Law which has served as a source of inspiration for national legislators, including the recent French legislation on the reform of the law of obligations of the French *Code civil*. Other groups of comparative lawyers have started work on principles of European tort law, family law, trust law, insurance law, and the law of civil procedure. There are now journals focusing on the development of European private

---

[12]Pound (1934), p. 168.

[13]For a thorough analysis and detailed references to the vast literature see, for example, Zimmermann (2006), p. 539; Reimann (2002), pp. 690–695.

[14]Reimann (2002), p. 691.

[15]See European Research Group on Existing EC Private Law (2009). For a critical evaluation of the Acquis Principles see Jansen and Zimmermann (2008).

law. Case books and comparative case studies have been published, and while there exist at this time no valid European rules on contract or tort law there are books which take the national rules as their starting point, and treat them as merely local variations of a European theme.[16]

It may be said therefore that the use of comparative law as a means to "Europeanize" the law is a success story. There is hardly a comparative project in Europe these days which does not see itself as a contribution to the Europeanization of private law. Nonetheless there is a fierce debate in Europe on where we should go from here. Some comparative lawyers have gone so far as to say that the preparation and introduction of a European Civil Code or at least a European Code of Contract Law are both feasible and desirable. Others have said that the unification of European contract law would be tolerable only to the extent to which it would be limited to the mandatory rules of consumer protection. This would in their view be essential for the proper functioning of the common market since businesses engaged in cross-border transactions with European consumers would be able to rely on uniform consumer protection rules. What would be unacceptable, however, is in their view the unification or harmonization of the general non-mandatory "dispositive" rules of contract law. Although he was for many years an active member of the "Commission of European Contract Law" Professor Roy Goode said that

> in the realm of general dispositive law there is much to be said for retaining the rich diversity of national legal systems, so that contracting parties have a wide range of choice and select their own law or that of another legal system with which they feel comfortable. European legal culture would be greatly impoverished if, at the level of fundamental principle and dispositive law, a singely set of rules were to be imposed on Member States.[17]

What about the great gulf supposedly existing between the Continental legal systems, on the one hand, and the English and Irish common law, on the other? Many scholars take the view that the discrepancies between the civil law and the common law have often been overrated. *Reinhard Zimmermann* thinks that the two systems are "no strangers",[18] *Basil Markesinis* observed a process of "gradual convergence",[19] and *James Gordley* called the old distinction "out-dated".[20] Others believe that the differences between these two "legal families" are unbridgeable and that the idea of "Europeanizing" the law is flawed and misconceived on this ground alone. *Pierre Legrand* takes the position that the law does not have a determinate content apart from a given culture and its specific mentalities, traditions, attitudes

---

[16]See, for example, Kötz (2017), von Bar (1998, 2000), Wagner (2003) and van Dam (2013).

[17]Quoted from the article by McKendrick (2006), p. 28. *Goode*'s views are supported by McKendrick himself. See also Beale (2006), p. 37 f.: He is also in favour of maintaining English contract law but thinks that in order to keep English law up-to-date and accessible in form much closer attention should be given to reform measures taken or proposed by Continental legal systems and the "Principles of European Contract Law". Beale has also been a member of the "Commission of European Contract law". Needless to say that these statements were made before the Brexit.

[18]See Zimmermann (2006), p. 558; Zimmermann (1996).

[19]Markesinis (1994, 2000).

[20]Gordley (1993).

and mind-sets. Since these differences and other cultural and linguistic barriers cannot be overcome, he thinks that the idea of the "convergence" of the civil law and the common law is unfounded, that the so-called "transplantation" of legal rules is unworkable in practice, and that the traditional approach of comparative law must be criticized because of its built-in bias towards the suppression of diversity, the diminution of particularity, and the denial of "*la différence*".[21] This is not the place to discuss the reasons why I think that *Legrand* may have overstated his case. Let me just say that the unification of French, Swiss and German law by the French, Swiss and German Civil Codes cannot be said to have been irrational on the sole ground that the mentality of lawyers in Marseille, Geneva and Munich differed—and perhaps differs even today—from the mentality of lawyers in Paris, Zürich and Hamburg. Doesn't the unification of international sales law make sense despite the fact that the Vienna Convention has meanwhile been ratified by some 80 countries and is applied without more ado by courts steeped in different traditions and speaking different languages?

Nonetheless, I do not think that we should now follow the request made several times already by the European Parliament "to bring into line the private law of the Member States"[22] by drawing up a "European Civil Code" or a "European Code of Contract Law". There is no clear competence for such a step at the European level, nor is there a political will in the Member States that would be needed to create such a competence. There is a European competence to unify or harmonize contract law to the extent to which it is intended to provide a mandatory protection for the consumer, and there is a lot to be said for taking further measures in this limited direction.[23] On the other hand, the time has not yet come to devise a set of uniform rules on non-mandatory contract law, let alone on tort or property law. There is the argument that a uniform set of contract rules will save the transaction costs arising in cross-border business deals if the parties have to seek certainty about the various possible national jurisdictions and agree on the law they think is most satisfactory. However, these costs are less important than generally assumed and will often be outweighed by the other costs of doing business abroad, such as the costs of complying with different tax regimes, different administrative requirements and differences of language, commercial customs and enforcement procedures. In addition, one must not

[21]See, for example, Legrand (1996a, b, c, 1997a, b). For a critical evaluation of *Legrand*'s thesis see, for example, Graziadei (2006), pp. 467–470.

[22]See the Resolution by the European Parliament of 26 May 1989 (OJ EC 1989 C 158/400).

[23]This does not mean, of course, that the "acquis communautaire" is sacrosanct. See the critical observations by Jansen and Zimmermann (2008). – In 2011 the EC issued a proposal for a Regulation on a Common European Sales Law (CESL) which would have been applicable to cross-border transactions for the sale of goods (and related agreements) provided that one party was either a consumer or a medium-sized business (as defined in the CESL). This proposal was withdrawn in 2014 due to the opposition of many Member States. This is perhaps regrettable. After all the CESL was intended to be an "optional instrument" that would have been applicable only if the parties had reached an agreement to that effect. It would have been interesting to see whether the CESL would have been able to successfully compete against the national rules on which the parties might also have agreed.

forget the cost of applying new uniform rules which would for a long time exist only on paper and would be untested by the courts or legal practice.

Nonetheless many comparative lawyers in Europe seem to take the position that any difference between the private laws of the Member States can be accused of standing in the way of the completion of the internal market and must, on that ground alone, be eliminated forthwith. There are at least two reasons why I cannot accept this statement. First, there is evidence showing that a single market can develop and flourish despite internal diversity of law. Second, I think that the time is not yet ripe for a unification or harmonization of general non-mandatory contract law.

There is little doubt that a country may have different systems of contract law and at the same time a perfectly functioning internal market. The United States and Canada are prime examples. Each of the 50 states of the American Union and each of the 11 Canadian provinces have jurisdiction over their civil law, and thus over contract law. It is true that there is uniform law to the extent that the federal legislature made use in these countries of the competence alloted to it under the constitution, and it is also true that individual states of provinces have in some cases seen fit to enact legislation based on a uniform model statute. But this occurs only where a uniform solution finds political support in the individual state or province and can be shown to be a manifest improvement of the law or as clearly required for a functioning common market. Given a system of reasonably uniform conflict of law rules legal diversity is accepted in these countries with a fair amount of equanimity. In Continental Europe and in the European Union, on the other hand, many lawyers take the position that the unification or harmonization of the law is meritorious and desirable *in itself* and should take place just for the sake of it even where there is no obvious and demonstrable need for it.[24]

Even if there existed a need for the unification of non-mandatory contract law I wonder if there is a sufficient consensus on the solutions to be adopted. It is true that the "Principles of European Contract Law" reflect a common understanding of the basic principles of contract law. There may be differences, however, on what these general principles actually mean in practical cases. It is all very well to say that contracting parties must act in accordance with "good faith and fair dealing", that they owe each other a "duty to co-operate" or that they are under a duty to volunteer information in the negotiation phase if that information is useful, important, material

[24]The United Kingdom is another example of a perfectly functioning single market despite significant differences between the legal systems of England and Scotland. A more detailed discussion of the point and of the reasons explaining the different approaches may be found in Kötz (2012) and Halberstam and Reimann (2014), pp. 41–45. Diversity of the law has also been supported on the ground that it allows the law of the states to compete with each other. The United States may therefore be seen "as a gigantic laboratory for legal policy in which any state can move forward in any direction by legislation or judicial decision and thus gain experience and reach views which enrich the debates on legal policy and may serve as an encouraging or horrifying example to other states". See Zweigert and Kötz (1998), p. 251. – "Regulatory competition" has also been held to have induced European law-makers to reform their contract law and dispute resolution mechanisms so as to attract parties to cross-border contracts to opt for the law and the courts of one country rather than another. See Kieninger (2012), p. 301; Vogenauer (2013).

or determinative for the other side. It is easy to say that a contract may be terminated in the event of a "change of circumstances" or of a breach of a time stipulation which the parties agreed to be "important" or to be "of the essence" of the contract. Few will dissent from such general principles, and they may well have been accepted in the civil codes of many Continental legal systems. There is nonetheless evidence showing that such general principles are susceptible to widely differing interpretations which depend on lawyers' traditional patterns of thought and frames of mind, on their working styles and methods of interpretation, on the different procedures applied by the courts in various countries, and on the type of contract usually litigated before the higher courts of a country.[25] It is certainly possible and indeed likely that the calls for a harmonization of "dispositive" contract law may increase in future years. What is needed in the present stage is not, however, to rush to uniform legislation on a European level. What is needed instead are further reforms of national contract law which follow the European trend.[26] We must also realize that uniform European legislation will only be workable in practice if the minds of European lawyers have been prepared for it by further comparative research and a thorough denationalization of legal education. What I just said may strike many as being unduly reserved and skeptical, especially since I am saying this as an *aficionado* of traditional comparative law which has often been accused—wrongly, I think—of a systematic bias towards "unity, harmony and gradual assimilation."[27] I hope, though, that this might make my statement more believable. After all, as the English mathematician *G.H. Hardy* once said: If the Archbishop of Canterbury says he believes in God, that's all in the way of business. But if he says he doesn't, you can take it he means what he says.

References

Ancel F, Fauvarque-Cosson B, Guest J (2017) Aux sources de la réforme du droit des contrats. Dalloz

Beale H (2006) English law reform and the impact of European private law. In: Vogenauer S, Weatherill S (eds) The harmonisation of European contract law. Hart, p 31 ff

Cooter R, Schäfer HB (2012) Solomon's knot, how law can end the poverty of nations. Princeton University Press

Dannemann G (2006) Comparative law: study of similarities and differences? In: Reimann M, Zimmermann R (eds) The Oxford handbook of comparative law. Oxford University Press, p 383 ff

European Research Group on Existing EC Private Law (Acquis Group) (ed) (2009) Principles of the existing EC Contract Law (Acquis Principles)

[25] The last-mentioned point is discussed more thoroughly by Kötz (1998), p. 256 f.

[26] The recent reform of the French law of contract is a good example. See Ancel et al. (2017).

[27] See Reimann (2002), p. 681.

Friedman L (1990) Some thoughts on comparative legal culture. In: Clark DS (ed) Comparative and private international law, essays in Honor of John Henry Merryman. Duncker and Humblot, p 49 ff
Gordley J (1993) Common law and civil law: Eine überholte Unterscheidung. Zeitschrift für Europäisches Privatrecht 1:498
Graziadei M (2006) Comparative law as the study of transplants and receptions. In: Reimann M, Zimmermann R (eds) The Oxford handbook of comparative law. Oxford University Press, p 441 ff
Halberstam D, Reimann M (2014) Federalism and legal unification: comparing methods, results, and explanations across 20 systems. In: Halberstam D, Reimann M (eds) Federalism and legal unification. Springer, p 3 ff
Jansen N, Zimmermann R (2008) Restating the Acquis Communautaire? A critical examination of the principles of the existing EC contract law. Mod Law Rev 71:505
Kieninger EM (2012) Competition between legal systems. In: Basedow J, Hopt K, Zimmermann R (eds) The Max Planck Encyclopedia of European private law. OUP, p 301
Kötz HD (1998) Towards a European civil code: the duty of good faith. In: Cane P, Stapleton J (eds) The law of obligations, essays in celebration of John Fleming. Oxford University Press, p 243 ff
Kötz HD (2012) Contract law in Europe and the United States: legal unification in the civil law and common law. Tulane Eur Civil Law Forum 27:1
Kötz HD (2017) European contract law, 2nd edn (trans: Weir T, Mertens G). Oxford University Press
Legrand P (1996a) How to compare now. Legal Stud 16:232
Legrand P (1996b) European legal systems are not converging. Int Comp Law Q 45:52
Legrand P (1996c) Sens et Non-sens d'un Code civil européen. Revue internationale de droit comparé 48:779
Legrand P (1997a) Against a European civil code. Mod Law Rev 60:44
Legrand P (1997b) The impossibility of legal transplants. Maastricht J Eur Comp Law 4:111
Markesinis B (1994) Learning from Europe and learning in Europe. In: Markesinis B (ed) The gradual convergence. Oxford University Press p 1 ff
Markesinis B (2000) The coming together of the common law and the civil law. Hart
Mckendrick E (2006) Harmonisation of European contract law: the state we are in. In: Vogenauer S, Weatherill S (eds) The harmonisation of European contract law. Hart, p 5 ff
Michaels R (2012) Comparative law. In: Basedow J, Hopt K, Zimmermann R (eds) The Max Planck Encyclopedia of European private law. OUP, p 297
Pound R (1934) The place of American law in the law school curriculum. Tulane Law Rev 8:161
Reimann M (1998) Stepping out of the European shadow: why comparative law in the United States must develop its own Agenda. Am J Comp Law 46:637
Reimann M (2002) The progress and failure of comparative law in the second half of the twentieth century. Am J Comp Law 50:671
Van Dam C (2013) European tort law, 2nd edn. Oxford University Press
Vogenauer S (2013) Regulatory competition through choice of contract law and choice of forum in Europe: theory and evidence. Eur Rev Private Law 21:13
Von Bar C (1998) The common European law of torts, vol 1. Clarendon Press
Von Bar C (2000) The common European law of torts, vol 2. Clarendon Press
Wagner G (2003) Grundstrukturen des Europäischen Deliktsrechts. In: Zimmermann R (ed) Grundstrukturen des Europäischen Deliktsrechts, p 189 ff
Zimmermann R (1996) Savigny's legacy: legal history, comparative law and the emergence of a European legal science. Law Q Rev 112:580
Zimmermann R (2006) Comparative law and the Europeanization of private law. In: Reimann M, Zimmermann R (eds) The Oxford handbook of comparative law. Oxford University Press, p 539 ff
Zweigert K, Kötz HD (1998) Introduction to comparative law, 3rd edn (trans: Weir T). Oxford University Press

Hein D. Kötz, un homme en marche

Bénédicte Fauvarque-Cosson

La joie de s'instruire est de tous les jours et de tous les âges. Ce goût peu à peu contracté, cet amour des livres, des idées, et du droit, nul ne les personnifie mieux que ces grands comparatistes auxquels nous rendons hommage. Ce goût *joyeux* de la connaissance, cher Professeur Kötz, vous l'incarnez, au sens propre et non seulement figuré. Votre marche reste celle d'un jeune homme et votre gourmandise pour le droit comparé est juvénile.

Ne vous donnez pas pour but d'être quelque chose, mais quelqu'un, écrivait Victor Hugo.

Qui êtes-vous donc, cher Professeur Kötz ? Reinhard Zimmermann, qui a eu le privilège de passer de nombreuses années à vos côtés à l'Institut Max Planck, a déjà dressé votre portrait : Hein D. Kötz « comme homme et comme scientifique, est unique, comparable à la rigueur à bien des égards à Konrad Zweigert et Gerhard Kegel : cosmopolite, serein, avec une distance ironique aux choses, avec de la répartie et adroit dans son jugement, curieux, original dans la forme, le style et le fond, avec le goût pour la formule percutante et doué d'un talent brillant, présentant des situations complexes de manière claire et élégante » (Hambourg, juin 2016).

Pour moi, Hein D. Kötz est le prince du droit comparé et du droit privé européen. Un prince toujours en marche.

Sa vie, HD Kötz l'a brièvement narrée dans un article intitulé « Une vie en tant que juriste non-dogmatique », paru dans la *Zeitschrift für Europäisches Privatrecht*. Hein D. Kötz y raconte son père aventurier ; son enfance à Hambourg ; sa formation dans une entreprise de l'industrie pétrolière ; ses études de droit ; les séminaires à Munich avec le professeur de droit romain, Wolfgang Kunkel ; ses années où il fut

B. Fauvarque-Cosson (✉)
Université Paris 2 Panthéon-Assas, Paris, France
e-mail: benedicte.fauvarque-cosson@u-paris2.fr

K. Boele-Woelki, D. P. Fernàndez Arroyo (eds.), *The Past, Present and Future of Comparative Law - Le passé, le présent et le futur du droit comparé*, Ius Comparatum – Global Studies in Comparative Law 29, https://doi.org/10.1007/978-3-319-93770-0_5

assistant au Max-Planck-Institut ; son mariage dans l'église de Blankenese avec, comme organiste, Konrad Zweigert ; le master de droit comparé à Ann Arbor dans le Michigan, la thèse d'habilitation, à Hambourg en 1970, le séjour aux Etats-Unis comme professeur invité à Chicago ; le choix d'une carrière scientifique en Allemagne à l'Université de Constance ; à la fin des années 1990, l'offre reçue du Président de l'époque de la Société Max-Planck, Reimar Lüst, de devenir le successeur de Zweigert. Hein D. Kötz y parle encore de l'Institut Max-Planck qu'il dirigea pendant 22 ans et où il a toujours son bureau, de ses activités à la commission de réforme du droit des obligations, de son séjour à Cambridge à la prestigieuse Chaire Goodhart, de la création de la Bucerius Law School dont il a été le premier directeur, de son cheminement vers l'économie du droit.

De l'œuvre, nul mieux que l'auteur lui-même ne peut en rendre compte, par ses écrits, ses actions, ses pensées et aussi par... ses omissions. « *Keine Festschrift »: pas de Mélanges.* Hein D. Kötz est un « fervent adepte de la ligue des anti-hommages » disait R Zimmermann. Sa modestie ne saurait seule expliquer ce refus. D'autres, également modestes, ont fini par céder à cette tradition des Mélanges car si la véritable supériorité s'accompagne naturellement de modestie, celle-ci doit être une juste appréciation de sa valeur personnelle. Des Mélanges eussent ainsi été une forme de justice vis-à-vis de soi et aussi d'autrui. Cette justice, Hein D. Kötz nous l'a rendue, à sa manière. Pas de Mélanges certes, mais un ouvrage qui porte ce titre improbable, si *kötzien* : *Undogmatisches* – « non dogmatique ».

Publié à l'occasion du 70e anniversaire de Hein D. Kötz. composé de vingt chapitres rédigés entre 1977 et 2003, *Undogmatisches* donne une idée de la variété des thèmes auxquels Kötz s'est intéressé au fil des ans : le style des décisions des cours suprêmes, le devenir d'un droit civil commun européen, les relations entre le droit comparé et l'histoire du droit, le sens de l'enseignement du droit, les anciennes et les nouvelles missions du droit comparé, l'influence de la common law sur la pratique contractuelle internationale, et, depuis les années 1990, des sujets d'économie du droit. Ainsi, loin de chercher par tous moyens à redonner une cohérence à son œuvre, Hein D. Kötz nous montre que la vie, y compris celle d'un grand maître, n'est que cheminement. Hein D. Kötz est un homme « en marche ».

Dans cet hommage trop bref, pour rendre compte de l'œuvre peu conventionnelle d'HD Kötz (n'est-ce pas là le privilège des comparatistes que de sortir des sentiers battus?), je ne mentionnerai que quelques morceaux choisis dans l'œuvre considérable d'HD Kötz, issus de ses deux derniers ouvrages.

Le premier est intitulé « droit allemand des contrats ». Cela pourrait sembler banal mais est en fait peu ordinaire, comme le révèle HD Kötz, dans l'avant-propos : « Chaque juriste étranger considèrerait comme la chose la plus naturelle du monde que la matière soit découpée de telle manière et non autrement. Il en est autrement en Allemagne. Jusqu'à aujourd'hui, il n'existait pas chez nous de manuel de droit des contrats. »

Le deuxième ouvrage porte sur le droit européen des contrats. C'est une mise à jour complétée d'une seconde partie du très célèbre « Flessner et Kötz ». L'humour de la préface est merveilleux : « Les auteurs disent rarement d'emblée que le sujet de leur livre n'existe pas. De fait, il n'existe rien de tel que le droit européen des contrats. Il n'est en vigueur nulle part et aucun juge, en Europe, ne l'appliquerait ». Quel panache ! C'est digne d'Edmond Rostand et de son célèbre Cyrano de Bergerac: *« Que dites-vous?...C'est inutile?... Je le sais! Mais on ne se bat pas dans l'espoir du succès !».* Le caractère novateur de la première édition de l'ouvrage a unanimement été salué et sa traduction, par Tony Weir, lui a assuré une diffusion mondiale. La deuxième édition est promise à une belle destinée mondiale : déjà traduite en anglais et en italien, elle le sera prochainement en français et dans de nombreuses autres langues. Récusant toute forme de dogmatisme juridique, l'ouvrage, accessible aux lecteurs de toutes nationalités, éveille le sens de la discussion; car ce qui intéresse Hein D. Kötz n'est pas de décrire les règles de droit en vigueur, comme un système fermé, logique et cohérent. Convaincu que ce sont des ordres juridiques nationaux qui fournissent la matière dont le droit européen des contrats sera fait, Hein D. Kötz nous donne les moyens de développer une compréhension commune du droit, par les droits nationaux, mais au-delà d'eux-mêmes. C'est pourquoi l'œuvre est non seulement stimulante mais séminale : elle inspirera toux ceux – qu'ils soient juges, praticiens, législateurs ou universitaires –, qui veulent construire l'Europe en partant de la comparaison des droits.

Partir des droits nationaux et, sur cette base, rechercher ardemment la dimension européenne du sujet : tel est le chemin de vie comparatiste dans lequel nous entraîne Hein D. Kötz. Hein D. Kötz, contrairement à d'autres, n'a pas combattu pour faire advenir le droit européen des contrats ni même un cadre commun de référence. Il s'est concentré sur ce qui n'existait pas. Et il l'a fait exister.

Loin du dogmatisme et du nationalisme juridiques, toute son œuvre, depuis la très célèbre *Introduction au droit comparé* coécrite avec Konrad Zweigert, pose les fondations les plus solides qui soient pour l'avènement d'un droit commun européen. Ce qu'Hein D. Kötz cherche à atteindre, n'est pas l'unification de façade, produite par une directive d'harmonisation maximale ou un règlement européen d'application directe. C'est la façon de penser traditionnelle des juristes, leur mode de travail, leur méthode d'interprétation de la loi, leurs choix éthiques, les processus par lesquels les cas d'espèce sont jugés par les tribunaux selon les traditions de tel ou tel Etat. C'était déjà cette démarche qui avait conduit Hein D. Kötz à relever le défi de la conception et coécriture de la première édition du *Ius Commune casebook for the common law of Europe* consacrée au droit européen des contrats, à partir d'arrêts et autres sources de référence, ou encore à créer et diriger la si prestigieuse Bucerius Law School.

Mieux se connaître, pour mieux comprendre d'où l'on vient et où l'on va : tel est l'apport, immense, de l'œuvre d'Hein D. Kötz, fécondée par un homme constamment en marche et un esprit s'ouvrant inlassablement aux idées.

Ayant commencé cet hommage en citant Victor Hugo, c'est en m'y référant de nouveau que je le terminerai. Le 21 août 1849, Victor Hugo, élu président du Congrès international de la Paix, prononçait un discours d'ouverture dont ce passage, gravé dans les esprits européens : « Un jour viendra où vous France, vous Russie, vous Italie, vous Angleterre, vous Allemagne, vous toutes, nations du continent, sans perdre vos qualités distinctes et votre glorieuse individualité, vous vous fondrez étroitement dans une unité supérieure, et vous constituerez la fraternité européenne, absolument comme la Normandie, la Bretagne, la Bourgogne, la Lorraine, l'Alsace, toutes nos provinces, se sont fondues dans la France. Un jour viendra où il n'y aura plus d'autres champs de bataille que les marchés s'ouvrant au commerce et les esprits s'ouvrant aux idées ».

Remerciements/Acknowledgments

Hein D. Kötz

Madame le Président, Mesdames et Messieurs,

L'Académie internationale de droit comparé a décidé d'honorer aujourd'hui cinq comparatistes dont je fais partie et je l'en remercie chaleureusement. Je ne vous cacherai pas que j'éprouve un immense plaisir à figurer parmi ces cinq personnalités bien que je ne sois pas tout à fait certain de mériter cette distinction.

Dans son éloge, Madame Fauvarque-Cosson a certes exposé les raisons qui lui semblent justifier cette décision. J'aimerais la remercier à son tour. Malgré l'élégance de son discours et son éloquence, elle n'a pas réussi toutefois à dissiper entièrement mes doutes. Je me sens un peu comme l'homme ayant atteint un certain âge, à qui l'on offrirait un recueil de mélanges. Si l'on en croit les mots du philosophe anglais Roger Collingword, de tels mélanges ne représentent rien d'autre que « la dernière humiliation faite à un savant par ses disciples, qui ont décidé de lui confectionner et de lui offrir un volume d'essais comme témoignage de sa sénilité ».

Nous sommes à Paris. Je vous prie, quand même, de bien vouloir m'excuser de poursuivre la discussion en anglais. En effet, l'usage du français n'est pas si aisé pour moi. Ma relation avec la langue française est un peu comme celle que j'entretiens avec ma femme : je l'aime assurément, mais je ne la domine pas. C'est pourquoi je ne veux pas vous faire l'affront de m'essayer la pratique de cette si belle langue devant vous.

À ce propos, une anecdote me vient à l'esprit : lors de la visite officielle de l'Empereur François-Joseph d'Autriche à Budapest en 1896, il fut accueilli par le Premier Ministre hongrois, le compte Bánffy, qui s'adressa à lui dans un allemand

H. D. Kötz (✉)
Max Planck Institute for Comparative and International Private Law, Hamburg, Germany
e-mail: koetz@mpipriv.de

K. Boele-Woelki, D. P. Fernàndez Arroyo (eds.), *The Past, Present and Future of Comparative Law - Le passé, le présent et le futur du droit comparé*, Ius Comparatum – Global Studies in Comparative Law 29, https://doi.org/10.1007/978-3-319-93770-0_6

calamiteux. L'Empereur d'Autriche avait immédiatement interrompu son interlocuteur en lui disant qu'il maîtrisait parfaitement le hongrois. Ce à quoi le comte Bánffy avait répondu: « Pas de proplème, Majestät: che dois toujours exxxercer ». C'est précisément ce supplice que je veux vous épargner à tout prix.

Partie III / Part III
Xavier Blanc-Jouvan

Le passé, le présent et l'avenir du droit comparé

Xavier Blanc-Jouvan

Ce n'est certes un secret pour personne que le droit comparé se trouve aujourd'hui à la croisée des chemins. Tandis que certains proclament qu'il a connu son âge d'or au XIXème siècle et sombrent dans le pessimisme en déplorant « la fin des héros »[1], d'autres, au contraire, remettent en cause l'héritage reçu et laissent entendre que l'ère du « vrai » droit comparé, si malmené jusqu'ici, n'a pas encore commencé[2]. Cette forme de crise d'identité est d'autant plus frappante qu'elle saisit le monde des juristes au moment même où un nombre croissant de ceux-ci, universitaires ou professionnels, semblent s'intéresser à cette discipline (qui a d'ailleurs fait une entrée remarquée dans les programmes d'enseignement) et acceptent ouvertement d'y voir une branche distincte de la « science du droit ». C'est sans aucun doute un état d'esprit nouveau qui se fait jour sous nos yeux et auquel les plus anciens d'entre nous ne peuvent qu'être infiniment sensibles: car, à l'inverse de l'époque où le droit comparé passait plutôt pour un art d'agrément, réservé à quelques rares voyageurs ou esthètes, il n'est plus grand monde aujourd'hui qui ne se considère peu ou prou comme un comparatiste. Aussi bien faut-il se réjouir que l'Académie internationale de droit comparé ait pris l'initiative d'une réflexion sur ce qui apparaît un peu comme un paradoxe, tout en situant clairement son propos dans le temps: « le passé, le présent et le futur du droit comparé ». Mais, puisque le présent n'est, au mieux, qu'un instant de raison, nous nous bornerons ici à un double volet, en évoquant rapidement l'héritage du passé avant d'esquisser quelques perspectives d'avenir.

---

[1]Markesinis (2003), spéc. p. 35 et s.

[2]L'idée se trouve en filigrane dans nombre d'écrits de Legrand (1999), 30, qui invite le lecteur à « comparer *autrement* ».

X. Blanc-Jouvan (✉)
Université de Paris 1 Panthéon-Sorbonne, Paris, France

K. Boele-Woelki, D. P. Fernàndez Arroyo (eds.), *The Past, Present and Future of Comparative Law - Le passé, le présent et le futur du droit comparé*, Ius Comparatum – Global Studies in Comparative Law 29, https://doi.org/10.1007/978-3-319-93770-0_7

1 L'HERITAGE DU PASSE

Du développement remarquable qu'a connu le droit comparé depuis le fameux Congrès de 1900 – et surtout depuis la fin de la Seconde Guerre mondiale en 1945 –, on peut certes tirer quelques enseignements utiles. Sans revenir sur un certain nombre de questions qui se sont posées au départ, par exemple sur la nature même du droit comparé (science ou méthode ?) ou sa dénomination (souvent critiquée), mais sont indiscutablement bien dépassées aujourd'hui, nous nous limiterons à celles qui, en dépit des apparences, continuent à nourrir quelques malentendus et, tout en évitant de rouvrir de vieux débats, nous grouperons nos observations sous trois rubriques (d'ailleurs étroitement liées) relatives au but, à l'objet et à la méthode du droit comparé.

1.1 Le but du droit comparé

Les fins que l'on peut assigner aux études comparatives (en dehors même de la plus évidente, qui est de permettre à chacun une meilleure compréhension de son propre système de droit) sont naturellement diverses et il n'est rien d'étonnant à ce qu'elles évoluent avec le temps. Le schéma le plus pertinent nous paraît être celui qui a été proposé par Marc Ancel et conduit à distinguer « les trois âges du droit comparé ».

Au départ, il est clair que celui-ci a rempli une fonction essentiellement utilitaire, en incitant le législateur comme les juges nationaux à rechercher au-delà des frontières, surtout dans les pays qui leur semblaient géographiquement ou culturellement assez proches, le moyen de réformer et d'améliorer leur propre droit. Il va de soi que, dans cette perspective, on s'intéressait par priorité aux différences existant entre les systèmes afin d'y trouver une source d'inspiration.

C'est seulement plus tard que les circonstances ont fait naître, chez les politiques comme chez les juristes, l'illusion d'un monde unifié – et le droit comparé s'est alors donné pour tâche d'encourager le mouvement qui se dessinait en ce sens. C'était l'idée dominante à l'époque du Congrès tenu à Paris en 1900, sous les auspices de la Société de législation comparée, et qui fut popularisée en France par des hommes comme Raymond Saleilles, pour qui le droit comparé avait pour but de « dégager de l'ensemble des institutions particulières un fond commun, ou tout au moins des points de rapprochement susceptibles de faire apparaître, sous la diversité apparente des formes, l'identité foncière de la vie juridique universelle », et Edouard Lambert, qui, dans son ouvrage de 1903 sur « *La fonction du droit civil comparé* », allait jusqu'à défendre le concept d'un « droit commun législatif » valable pour toute l'humanité ou, du moins, celle que l'on disait, ou croyait, « civilisée »: le droit comparé devait ainsi jouer un rôle quasi normatif – ce qui supposait naturellement que l'accent fût mis sur la recherche des ressemblances. Bien qu'ayant survécu à la « Grande Guerre » (la période qui a suivi a même été celle de la création de nombreuses institutions ou organisations internationales destinées à progresser dans cette voie et allant de la Société des nations ou de l'Institut pour l'unification du droit privé de Rome, plus connu sous le nom d'Unidroit, à l'Académie internationale de droit comparé, dont chacun sait qu'elle est née en 1924), le rêve s'est heurté aux dures réalités de la Seconde Guerre mondiale et de la « guerre froide » qui s'en est suivie et donc quelque temps estompé, mais il n'en a pas moins réapparu dans la seconde moitié du siècle, bien qu'à une échelle plus modeste, pour les besoins de la construction européenne, avec la recherche d'un nouveau *jus commune*.

On peut pourtant se demander si, là encore, les choses n'ont pas déjà commencé à changer et si les recherches visant à la découverte d'un fond commun ont encore un sens à un moment où beaucoup estiment que la diversité est une richesse qu'il convient de préserver et où l'évolution semble s'orienter moins vers une unification globale des droits que vers une harmonisation (voire un simple rapprochement) à l'échelle régionale. Une autre vision s'est ainsi fait jour, qui conduit à assigner au droit comparé la fonction infiniment plus humble de permettre une meilleure compréhension entre les peuples et donc une meilleure entente entre les nations. Sans doute dois-je avouer que je ne partage pas tout à fait le scepticisme de ceux qui ne voient dans une telle conception que la marque d'un « sentimentalisme doucereux »[3]: pour avoir pas mal voyagé sur les cinq continents, je puis attester que l'intérêt que je portais à leur droit m'a souvent permis de nouer avec chacun des pays visités des liens plus étroits, car on aime toujours mieux ce que l'on comprend bien. Marc Ancel, qui avait lui-même des amis partout dans le monde, en était plus que quiconque convaincu – et ce n'est sans doute pas par hasard que tous les grands comparatistes que j'ai connus étaient en même temps de parfaits humanistes. Le droit comparé est certainement un remède contre toutes les formes de dogmatisme, de chauvinisme et d'ethnocentrisme – et force est d'admettre qu'à ce seul titre, sa fonction est déjà loin d'être négligeable.

Ce qui est vrai, pourtant, c'est qu'il serait dangereux de s'en tenir à ces seules finalités pratiques, qui risqueraient de nous faire oublier la vocation scientifique du droit comparé – et c'est ce que Rodolfo Sacco a eu justement le mérite de nous rappeler en nous livrant ce bel ouvrage dont le titre se suffit à lui seul : « *La comparaison juridique au service de la connaissance du droit* ». Tout est dit en quelques mots, surtout si l'on garde présent à l'esprit qu'il s'agit bien du droit en général et non pas seulement d'un droit particulier, le sien propre ou celui des autres: car le droit comparé, notamment par l'élaboration et la présentation de « modèles », apparaît, au même titre que l'histoire, par exemple, ou la sociologie, comme partie intégrante de la science du droit, au point de n'avoir besoin d'aucune autre justification que celle-ci.

Pas davantage n'est-il nécessaire de préciser que toutes ces fins peuvent coexister, voire se superposer (comme on l'a encore vu en France avec la dernière réforme du droit des contrats), de sorte que chacun de ceux qui s'engagent dans cette voie peut y trouver son compte. Il arrive simplement que l'une ou l'autre apparaisse comme prioritaire à une époque particulière, et c'est ce qui peut donner l'impression d'une

[3]Sacco (1991), 6.

succession de phases diverses. Tout au plus faut-il admettre que chacune influe à sa manière sur l'objet comme sur la méthode de la recherche à opérer dans ce domaine.

1.2 L'objet du droit comparé

Cet objet n'a cessé de s'étendre, aussi bien en ce qui concerne les matières couvertes (ce sont aujourd'hui toutes les branches du droit, y compris le droit public, où la discipline a même connu à l'époque récente, un remarquable essor) que les pays ou ordres juridiques considérés (il n'en est, bien sûr, aucun qui lui échappe), le niveau de la comparaison (dans la mesure où l'on oppose couramment la macro-comparaison, portant sur l'ensemble d'un système ou d'un ordre juridique, voire d'une branche du droit, à la micro-comparaison, qui ne s'intéresse qu'à une règle particulière ou une institution) ou ses modalités (puisqu'elle peut être bilatérale ou multilatérale, voire globale). Mais ce ne sont là que de banales constatations, sur lesquelles il convient d'autant moins de s'arrêter que le droit comparé implique la diversité et qu'il faut laisser à chacun la liberté de choisir son champ d'étude. Il ne reste en fait que deux questions pratiques sur lesquelles l'opinion continue à diverger assez sensiblement pour qu'il nous paraisse utile d'en dire ici un mot très rapide.

La première concerne la fameuse distinction qui avait été faite dès le Congrès de 1900 et a souvent été reprise depuis lors entre les études de droit comparé et celles portant simplement sur le droit étranger. Même si cette présentation se révèle parfaitement justifiée sur le terrain de la logique, le doute commence à apparaître lorsqu'on en vient à se demander s'il faut en déduire que tel ou tel de nos ouvrages classiques sur les grands systèmes de droit, voire telle thèse rédigée en France sur le *trust* en droit anglais ou la *Mitbestimmung* en droit du travail allemand, ne relève pas vraiment du droit comparé. Ce serait évidemment absurde et l'on est bien obligé d'en revenir à la saine raison. Il ne suffit pas de dire que, de toute façon, l'analyse du droit étranger est le préalable nécessaire de la comparaison. Il faut aller plus loin et admettre que, ne serait-ce qu'en raison de la différence des concepts d'un système à l'autre, elle implique déjà, pour pouvoir être comprise par les juristes d'un pays donné, un minimum de comparaison avec le droit de ce pays ou un autre droit déjà connu – faute de quoi elle sera parfaitement inintelligible et ne constituera jamais qu'une simple description, voire une juxtaposition de règles, du type de ces « tableaux comparatifs » que l'on trouve parfois dans certaines publications spécialisées et qui sont évidemment dépourvus de toute valeur scientifique ! Tout ce que l'on peut dire est qu'il y a place pour différents types d'approche suivant le but visé en même temps qu'il y a, bien sûr, des degrés possibles, voire une échelle, dans la comparaison: et il serait aussi injuste de ne pas laisser à chacun le choix de son registre que de prononcer sur ce point une quelconque exclusive. Il apparaît donc que la distinction n'a guère d'intérêt pratique et que l'accent parfois mis sur elle traduit une certaine méconnaissance de la matière. Je pense personnellement que l'on se trouve là en présence du type même de faux débat.

Une autre question classique est celle de savoir s'il convient, dans la comparaison proprement dite, d'insister sur les ressemblances ou, au contraire, sur les différences existant entre les systèmes considérés : on parle ainsi de comparaison « intégrative » par rapport à la comparaison « contrastée » ou « différentielle »[4]. Sur ce point, nous avons déjà noté l'évolution qui s'était produite depuis un peu plus de deux siècles en liaison avec les buts successivement assignés au droit comparé: c'est ainsi qu'on est passé, au moins sur notre continent, de la promotion d'un *jus commune* fondé sur le droit romain à la recherche des différences (au lendemain des grandes codifications), puis, à nouveau, dans le climat d'internationalisme qui prévalait vers 1900, à celle des ressemblances. Et même si ce dernier mouvement bénéficie encore d'une certaine faveur entourant les projets d'unification ou d'harmonisation internationale des droits, force est bien de constater que certains excès l'ont amené à s'essouffler quelque peu. Car il est vrai qu'on a vu se développer, au moins dans le cadre européen, une forme de prosélytisme tendant à exagérer cette quête des similitudes au risque de «forcer» quelque peu la réalité (certains ont parlé de « manipulation ») pour mieux atteindre un objectif qu'on s'est préalablement fixé : et la comparaison a quelquefois été confondue, bien à tort, avec la recherche effrénée de l'unification. Mais l'accord semble se faire aujourd'hui pour admettre que, quel que soit le but «politique» visé, le droit comparé en tant qu'activité scientifique se doit d'être neutre et de considérer sur un pied de parfaite égalité ce qui unit les systèmes de droit et ce qui les distingue, sans préférence ni exclusion (même si l'entente sur ce point paraît quelquefois plus facile à réaliser en théorie qu'à respecter en pratique): car les ressemblances sont aussi instructives que les différences. Cela doit donc conduire à faire preuve s'une grande prudence à l'égard de toutes les formes de « comparaison militante ». Celle-ci ne peut que nuire gravement à la cause du droit comparé.

Mais l'idée même de science nous renvoie bien vite à la question de la méthode – une question que nous ne pouvons ignorer, puisque c'est celle qui continue à susciter aujourd'hui, dans le cénacle comparatiste, la plus abondante littérature.

1.3 La méthode du droit comparé

Toute science requiert, en effet, une méthode, même si, pour éviter un terme qui évoque parfois l'existence d'un cadre rigide, on se borne parfois à parler ici d'approche : et l'on conçoit que celle qui prévaut en droit comparé présente, malgré quelques similitudes, bien des particularités par rapport à celle que l'on pratique en droit interne, notamment dans l'interprétation de la loi. Parce que, là encore, la voie à suivre dépend largement du but visé, il n'est pas étonnant qu'une évolution se soit produite et que l'on ait vu se succéder plusieurs écoles.

---

[4]V., not., pour une position très marquée sur ce problème, Legrand (1999), 37: « Il y a lieu [...] de comprendre que le comparatisme en droit ne saurait avoir pour raison d'être que l'appréhension des différences ».

L'approche initiale, et la plus simpliste, dite textuelle, a été, au moins dans les pays de « droit civil » et dans la ligne de l'Exégèse, celle qui reposait sur l'analyse des textes : on pensait que, pour connaître le droit d'un pays, il suffisait de consulter ses codes – en s'appuyant au besoin sur l'intention du législateur. En dehors du fait qu'elle n'a guère eu l'occasion de faire ses preuves, puisqu'à l'époque, on se souciait assez peu des droits étrangers, tout le monde admet aujourd'hui que la méthode est à la fois insuffisante (quand il n'y a pas de texte) et trompeuse (quand le texte ne traduit pas exactement la réalité du droit). Elle ne peut donc conduire qu'à une comparaison purement superficielle et se trouve, de ce fait, largement dépassée.

La vraie comparaison est née un peu plus tard, au moment même où se développait, dans les pays d'influence germanique, l'approche conceptuelle du droit : et celle-ci s'est naturellement étendue au droit comparé. La comparaison devait alors porter exclusivement sur l'analyse des concepts et la recherche de notions juridiques communes. Mais le mouvement qui s'est ainsi fait jour, en Allemagne comme au dehors, au lendemain de la promulgation du BGB, et qui a connu un grand succès dans toute une partie de l'Europe, ne pouvait séduire ceux des juristes qui ne partageaient pas le même goût pour l'abstraction ou restaient attachés aux particularités juridiques nationales : et c'est ce qui explique son relatif déclin, encore qu'on en retrouve des traces non négligeables dans une certaine doctrine contemporaine et dans le regain d'intérêt pour les concepts qui tend aujourd'hui à se manifester çà et là, sans doute en réaction contre une pression trop forte de la *common law*.

Il a fallu attendre la fin de la Seconde Guerre mondiale pour que triomphent à l'échelle internationale les vues développées en Allemagne par Ernst Rabel (« le père du fonctionnalisme »), puis acclimatées aux Etats-Unis par des disciples tels que Rudolf Schlesinger et Max Rheinstein et finalement répandues (au moins en droit privé) sur les cinq continents. En partant du concept de « comparabilité » et en se fondant sur l'idée que « dans le droit, les seules choses comparables sont celles qui remplissent les mêmes fonctions », ces pionniers ont mis l'accent sur la fonction que remplissent les règles ou les institutions : et il en est résulté une approche dite « fonctionnelle » qui, même si elle a connu quelques avatars, chacun cherchant naturellement à lui ajouter ou lui soustraire quelque chose, n'en est pas moins devenue la plus couramment acceptée et la plus largement utilisée dans les milieux comparatistes. Rappelons seulement qu'elle a inspiré des travaux de grande qualité, comme le projet de recherches sur « *le fond commun des systèmes juridiques* », conduit à la *Cornell Law School* vers le début des années 1960 sous la direction de Schlesinger et avec le concours de juristes tels que Gino Gorla. Elle présente trois caractères essentiels. D'abord, c'est une approche empirique et concrète, qui met l'accent sur les faits de l'espèce et se situe dans une perspective quasi utilitaire du droit, où l'on retrouve nettement l'influence de la *common law*. Le point de départ de la comparaison est moins la norme considérée en elle-même – qu'il s'agisse des « mots de la loi » ou du concept qui la sous-tend – que la manière dont elle est mise en œuvre dans la pratique (« *the law in action* »). L'attention se porte donc par priorité sur les « cas » et la jurisprudence. Ensuite, c'est une approche déjà contextuelle dans la mesure où elle implique que chaque norme individuelle soit replacée dans l'ensemble du système et dans son contexte juridique, en tenant compte notamment des fameuses lois de compensation ou de substitution bien connues de tous les comparatistes. Enfin, c'est une approche qui privilégie la recherche des ressemblances entre les systèmes de droit et repose même sur une véritable « présomption de similitude » (*praesumptio similitudinis*), du fait que les fonctions à remplir et les besoins à satisfaire sont censés être à peu près les mêmes dans toutes les sociétés, du moins lorsque celles-ci sont culturellement assez proches. Rien ne semble alors s'opposer à la découverte d'un « *common core* »...

Cette méthode a pourtant elle aussi essuyé le feu de la critique et, tout en reconnaissant ses avantages (notamment son pragmatisme), certains n'ont pas manqué d'émettre quelques réserves, qui vont d'ailleurs dans des sens assez différents, sinon inverses. Sur le plan pratique, on a par exemple regretté le recours trop fréquent à une approche purement factuelle, qui détourne l'attention des concepts pourtant indispensables au développement de la science du droit (notamment dans les pays romanistes, où l'art d'abstraire demeure une vertu cardinale), en même temps que la place trop grande faite à cette présomption de ressemblance qui amène parfois à se satisfaire d'une analyse un peu superficielle et qui, de toute façon, paraît plus facile à mettre en œuvre en droit privé qu'en droit public, où les divergences sont naturellement plus grandes d'un pays à l'autre. Sur le plan de la théorie générale du droit, et tout en s'attaquant à la notion même de fonction (qui ne suffit pas à leurs yeux à caractériser une règle de droit), des critiques ont fait valoir que le fonctionnalisme était au fond plus positiviste que réaliste en ce qu'il se concentre encore trop sur les normes au risque de laisser de côté certains grands problèmes et de ne pas apporter de réponse aux questions qui se posent, par exemple, dans la comparaison entre systèmes juridiques radicalement différents.

Mais voilà que nous touchons justement à un problème relativement nouveau du droit comparé – et donc au « futur » de notre discipline. Il nous reste à envisager rapidement les principales perspectives d'avenir qui se dessinent aujourd'hui.

2 LES PERSPECTIVES D'AVENIR

L'avenir, en fait, a déjà commencé et il serait bien imprudent de vouloir prédire ce qu'il nous réserve. Nous nous limiterons donc ici à un constat et un projet: car on ne peut guère douter que l'un des principaux défis auxquels va se trouver confrontée notre discipline sera celui de la mondialisation, et c'est pour y faire face que nous devrons concentrer nos efforts sur la formation des futurs comparatistes. Il s'agit là de deux questions cruciales sur lesquelles on nous permettra de nous en tenir à quelques brèves observations.

2.1 *Le défi de la mondialisation*

Qu'on le veuille ou non, il faut bien constater aujourd'hui que la mondialisation est un fait, une réalité que l'on n'a pas plus à accepter qu'à refuser, car elle fait partie d'une évolution, de la technique comme des mentalités, sur laquelle nulle autorité n'a de prise et nul Etat ne peut songer à revenir. Sans vouloir céder à aucun effet de mode sur ce point, on ne peut manquer de reconnaître l'importance qu'elle présente dans le domaine du droit – et notamment du droit comparé : car le phénomène affecte aussi bien les systèmes juridiques eux-mêmes que la structure, l'objet et les méthodes de la comparaison.

La première évidence est, en effet, qu'en entraînant un rapprochement, sinon un véritable brassage des différents systèmes juridiques, la mondialisation ouvre très largement la voie à cette « mixité » (entendue au sens le plus large du terme) qui est l'une des caractéristiques majeures du droit contemporain – et dont chacun a bien conscience qu'elle ne peut aller qu'en s'affirmant chaque jour davantage. D'ores et déjà, on peut constater qu'elle aboutit à remettre en cause la notion classique de « famille juridique » en même temps qu'elle relance le vieux débat sur une prétendue « convergence des droits », dans laquelle il est permis de ne voir que le paravent d'une véritable domination de certains droits sur les autres (en partie grâce à la généralisation de cette *lingua franca* qu'est devenu l'anglais). Ce qui est certain, en tout cas, est qu'on assiste à une interpénétration croissante des systèmes juridiques et que des phénomènes comme les migrations de droits ou la circulation de modèles prennent de plus en plus d'ampleur. Qui peut nier aujourd'hui l'existence d'une sorte de marché international du droit, sur lequel s'exerce de plus en plus une véritable « concurrence des droits » ? Il y aurait évidemment beaucoup à dire sur tous ces thèmes, qui mériteraient d'être examinés de façon plus approfondie. Que l'on pense seulement au fameux rapport « *Doing Business* » de la Banque mondiale, qui a fait tant de bruit il y a quelques années dans le monde du *civil law*, et à l'impulsion très forte qu'il a donnée à la comparaison inter-systémique dans un climat particulièrement compétitif !

Et voilà que cette dernière remarque nous amène précisément à notre second point : car l'évolution en cours ne s'arrête pas là, et la mondialisation emporte aussi des conséquences en ce qui concerne le processus même de la comparaison. Chacun conçoit qu'en conduisant à une multiplication des échanges internationaux, elle rend plus nécessaire que jamais la connaissance des droits étrangers. Mais son effet se traduit plus particulièrement à deux égards.

D'abord, elle entraîne l'apparition, à l'échelle internationale ou supranationale, de nouvelles sources de droit qui viennent se superposer à l'Etat-nation, puisqu'aussi bien celui-ci n'a plus aujourd'hui le monopole de la création du droit et que rien n'empêche le développement d'un véritable pluralisme juridique sur un territoire donné. Or il va de soi que tous ces ordres juridiques nouveaux, qui font concurrence au droit étatique, entrent dans le champ du droit comparé : ils élargissent donc sensiblement son domaine en même temps qu'ils rendent la comparaison plus complexe, en ce qu'elle ne se déroule plus simplement sur un plan horizontal, mais entre des systèmes et à des niveaux différents.

Mais la mondialisation contribue aussi à élargir le champ de la comparaison en l'étendant, au nom de l'universalisme de la science juridique, même à des systèmes « radicalement différents », dont l'étude a longtemps relevé plutôt d'autres disciplines telles que l'ethnologie ou l'anthropologie. Alors que, traditionnellement, l'intérêt des juristes se concentrait, en fait, sur des pays proches ou voisins (ce qui apparaissait comme une manifestation de l'ethnocentrisme ambiant : on a même parlé d'européocentrisme), il tend aujourd'hui à se porter aussi sur tous ces droits que, dans le classement en familles juridiques, on se bornait jadis à regrouper dans une grande famille, un peu résiduelle, des « droits traditionnels ou religieux ». Si bienvenue soit-elle, cette extension géographique n'est pourtant pas sans poser quelques problèmes nouveaux aux comparatistes, dans la mesure où la bonne compréhension d'un droit implique nécessairement celle du milieu dans lequel il s'enracine.

Chacun connaît la position prise à cet égard par le courant de pensée postmoderniste qui, par principe et au nom du relativisme culturel, émet des doutes sur la possibilité même d'une authentique comparaison lorsque l'observateur se trouve confronté à des systèmes avec lesquels il n'a, au départ, aucune véritable affinité. Pierre Legrand pose directement la question : « Si les cadres linguistiques, épistémologiques, éthiques et culturels des droits sont différents, les chercheurs étrangers peuvent-ils vraiment les comprendre et les comparer ? ». La réponse semble alors s'imposer : ce que décrivent ces chercheurs est moins la réalité de ces droits que la représentation qu'ils s'en font. D'où la conclusion, qui a d'ailleurs une portée générale, suivant laquelle, faute de repères objectifs, de concepts adéquats et de langage commun, les droits sont à proprement parler incommensurables et la comparaison entre eux ne peut être qu'« anodine » ou « reposante », voire simplement « blafarde », en tout cas sans valeur scientifique. Cette position, sans être tout à fait nouvelle, comporte d'ailleurs une part de vérité : car chacun peut constater combien il est difficile, quand on étudie un droit étranger, de se défaire de certains préjugés issus de son propre système et d'atteindre à une parfaite objectivité. C'est pourquoi il est toujours nécessaire de jeter un regard critique sur certaines analyses trop légères ou hâtives, notamment quand elles entendent conduire à une intégration normative : il y a des limites à la comparaison et les mises en garde sont toujours utiles à cet égard. Mais il importe aussi de ne pas se montrer trop négatif : et c'est quand elles sont poussées à bout que les thèses postmodernistes se révèlent aussi excessives que dangereuses, car elles conduisent à nier la légitimité d'une science qui, sans prétendre à la perfection, a tout de même largement fait jusqu'ici la preuve de son utilité – et elles débouchent sur un scepticisme dévastateur.

Aussi bien faut-il revenir sur terre et admettre que bien des écueils ici relevés peuvent être évités par le recours à une méthode adéquate – et c'est justement ce qui a amené certains comparatistes à proposer un aménagement de l'approche fonctionnelle jusqu'ici couramment pratiquée. L'idée de départ est que plus le pays dont il cherche à comprendre le droit est différent du sien propre, plus l'observateur doit tenir compte dans sa vision et dans son interprétation des traditions et de la mentalité propres à la société concernée. En fait, le droit (et cela vaut aussi bien pour les normes imposées par l'autorité que pour les décisions rendues par les juges) ne prend tout son sens que si on le replace dans son contexte tant historique que religieux, idéologique, politique, économique et social. Et si la remarque vaut déjà lorsqu'un Français étudie le droit belge ou anglais, combien plus se vérifie-t-elle encore lorsqu'il s'intéresse à celui de la Chine, de la Nouvelle-Guinée ou de la République malgache ! Comment pourrait-on parler du « droit de l'Afrique sub-saharienne », pour autant que l'expression ait un sens, sans évoquer le passé colonial et la marque laissée par l'ancien colonisateur, français ou anglais, belge ou portugais, ou sans tenir compte du fossé qui continue à exister entre le droit étatique et le droit coutumier, la « loi sur le mariage » et l'authentique vie familiale, l'économie officielle (celle de l'OHADA…) et celle qui se pratique dans les villages le jour du marché, etc. ? Et c'est ainsi que s'est développée en droit comparé l'idée d'une « approche contextuelle » qui, sans répudier le « noyau dur » du fonctionnalisme (notamment son attachement aux situations de fait), le complète (et le corrige) en prenant plus de distance à l'égard des normes et de leur fonction, en renonçant même, quand il le faut, à la présomption de ressemblance et en faisant appel plus largement à tout le contexte qui entoure le droit[5]. On peut aussi qualifier cette méthode de « culturelle » dans la mesure où elle considère le droit avant tout comme un phénomène de culture, traduisant au mieux l'âme d'un peuple (le *Volksgeist*) : en utilisant toutes les ressources de l'herméneutique, elle favorise une démarche très pragmatique, qui est d'ailleurs celle de bien des comparatistes, et semble même aller de soi dans la mesure où elle fait toute sa place à l'intuition et à l'expérience, voire, pour parler en termes pascaliens, à l'esprit de finesse plutôt qu'à celui de géométrie. On pourrait même suggérer qu'elle suppose une certaine empathie de l'observateur à l'égard de l'objet étudié s'il ne s'agissait là d'une vertu qui, à la différence de la notion de comparabilité, ne s'apprend pas nécessairement dans les livres…

Ceci ne doit pas nous empêcher pourtant de songer à d'autres mesures qui pourraient aussi être prises pour mieux assurer l'avenir du droit comparé et qui consisteraient justement à améliorer autant que faire se peut la formation des futurs comparatistes : c'est bien le moins que l'on puisse attendre, en ce domaine, d'un universitaire…

2.2 La formation des comparatistes

Rien n'était jadis prévu pour former les juristes au droit comparé : en fait, c'était essentiellement affaire de circonstances – et l'on n'avait d'autre ressource que de s'improviser comparatiste ! Ce fut en tout cas mon expérience et je ne pense pas qu'elle ait été unique. Quand je suis parti au milieu du siècle dernier pour passer une

---

[5]Kischel (2016), 907 et s.

année à Cornell, je ne savais strictement rien de ce qu'était la *common law* et je n'ai pas eu connaissance d'un seul ouvrage d'introduction au droit des Etats-Unis qui fût alors, en France, à la portée d'un étudiant : j'ai donc dû tout apprendre sur le tas ! Les choses ont heureusement bien changé et l'on a pris conscience de ce que, dans la mesure où le droit comparé constitue aujourd'hui une discipline reconnue, le problème de la formation se pose en des termes de plus en plus pressants. Mais tout n'est pas réglé pour autant et, si d'immenses progrès ont déjà été réalisés sur ce terrain, on peut penser qu'il y a encore place pour quelques améliorations notables.

Une question préalable ne manque pas de surgir, et c'est celle de savoir s'il convient de faire du « droit comparé » une matière distincte ou de l'intégrer, au contraire, dans l'enseignement du droit national, comme cela se fait déjà pour d'autres sciences humaines ou sociales. Il s'agirait, au fond, de présenter aux étudiants les grands problèmes qui se posent avant d'envisager avec eux les différentes solutions possibles – un peu, justement, dans une perspective fonctionnaliste. L'idée est naturellement séduisante, dans la mesure où, tendant à développer chez tous une sorte de « réflexe comparatif », elle correspond le mieux à la vocation réelle du droit comparé, qui est d'imprégner l'ensemble du système juridique : elle évite de marginaliser la discipline aussi bien que ceux qui s'y adonnent, en faisant nécessairement de tout juriste un comparatiste. Mais elle soulève tant de difficultés d'ordre pratique que l'on peut douter de la possibilité de la mettre effectivement en œuvre : outre la nécessité de s'en tenir alors à quelques vagues généralités (car le domaine à couvrir est pratiquement illimité), elle risque de jeter la confusion dans l'esprit d'étudiants menacés d'une sorte de « schizophrénie juridique » (« Quel est mon droit?... »). Sans doute la méthode est-elle plus facile à envisager dans des institutions à vocation proprement internationale, qui ont vu le jour ici ou là pour enseigner le *global law* à des étudiants déjà avancés sans être elles-mêmes tenues par un programme précis, ou dans les pays de *common law*, où l'on enseigne le droit à partir de cas concrets, que dans le monde romaniste, où l'accent est naturellement mis sur les règles – encore que, même dans ce cas, on puisse y recourir plus facilement dans certaines matières, comme, par exemple, les conflits de lois ou le droit constitutionnel, où elle n'est d'ailleurs pas inconnue, que dans d'autres, où l'on est bien obligé de partir des codes... Je suis, pour ma part, assez réservé quant à la possibilité de l'utiliser de manière générale en droit civil ou commercial : et je ne puis m'empêcher de constater que, même dans les pays de droit mixte, où l'on doit bien enseigner dans le même établissement deux, voire plusieurs systèmes de droit, on le fait normalement par des cours distincts – ce qui n'est pas vraiment la perspective comparative à laquelle nous songeons ici.

Force apparaît donc finalement de se rabattre sur l'autre solution, qui consiste tout simplement à organiser des cours spéciaux de droit comparé, pouvant avoir un objet très divers : et je ne puis présenter à cet égard que quelques suggestions très rapides, en me limitant naturellement au cas de la France. Car, bien sûr, on ne peut tout faire en ce domaine et une spécialisation est nécessaire, aussi bien du côté de l'Université que de l'étudiant lui-même. Tout au plus me paraît-il indispensable de prévoir dès le début des études juridiques (c'est-à-dire, si possible, dès la première année – ce qui n'est pratiquement jamais le cas aujourd'hui) un cours obligatoire portant sur les grands systèmes de droit, leur histoire et leurs caractéristiques fondamentales (dans la ligne de la « systémologie » prônée par Rodolfo Sacco), afin de présenter aux étudiants une vue générale de la matière. Ce cours, dont on a dit parfois qu'il était un peu daté, m'apparaît au contraire comme tout à fait essentiel, surtout dans les pays où l'on aime encore les grandes synthèses, car il permet d'aller tout de suite aux fondamentaux et de toucher à nombre de problèmes relevant de la théorie générale du droit : il doit, en somme, faire partie de la « culture générale » de tout juriste. Au surplus, il devrait servir à capter l'intérêt des étudiants et leur donner les bases dont ils auront besoin pour s'orienter ensuite parmi les autres enseignements comparatifs, nécessairement optionnels, qui leur seront offerts au cours de leurs études, en fonction des moyens dont dispose l'Université, et seront, par la force des choses, limités à une ou plusieurs matières prises globalement (comme, par exemple, le droit pénal, le droit administratif ou le droit du travail) ou à un ou plusieurs systèmes déterminés (droit anglais, italien ou allemand[6]). Enfin, ce n'est qu'à un stade plus avancé de leur parcours, au niveau de la maîtrise ou du doctorat, qu'il y aurait lieu d'organiser des enseignements portant sur des thèmes plus précis et qui, en fait, devraient constituer surtout une initiation à la recherche. Faut-il préciser encore, pour répondre à une objection souvent présentée, que l'alourdissement des programmes résultant de tous ces cours nouveaux de « droit comparé » *lato sensu* pourrait, le cas échéant, être compensé, soit par la suppression de certains cours traditionnels qui ne sont plus aujourd'hui aussi nécessaires qu'ils ont pu l'être autrefois, soit par certaines réformes conduisant à sacrifier, même dans des matières concernant le droit national, des développements à caractère essentiellement réglementaire ou à portée purement contingente au profit de tout ce qui touche aux principes ou à l'esprit des institutions ?

Point n'est besoin, d'ailleurs, de s'appesantir sur ce sujet puisque le schéma ici esquissé correspond à celui qui existe déjà, au moins en filigrane, dans certains établissements et y fonctionne en pratique de façon satisfaisante. Encore pourrait-on s'attacher à créer un climat qui pousserait davantage les étudiants à profiter des possibilités qui leur sont ainsi offertes, soit en multipliant les mesures d'incitation (par exemple, en faisant mieux valoir auprès d'eux l'intérêt d'une formation au droit comparé pour leur avenir professionnel), soit en leur apportant une aide plus ciblée (notamment pour l'apprentissage des langues, si crucial en la matière: on me dira que cela est déjà fait aujourd'hui, mais je ne suis pas sûr qu'il n'y ait pas encore quelques progrès à réaliser dans ce domaine. . .). Surtout, il me semble nécessaire d'accroître les facilités qui leur sont accordées, mais ne sont pas encore suffisantes à bien des égards, pour poursuivre une partie de leurs études à l'étranger, soit dans le cours

[6]Me permettra-t-on de préciser que je crois particulièrement formateur, pour les étudiants des pays de tradition « romano-germanique », et même en dehors de toute considération d'ordre strictement professionnel, d'être initiés aux droits de *common law*, tant ceux-ci relèvent d'une vision vraiment différente du droit en même temps qu'ils ouvrent l'accès à d'autres modes de pensée et de raisonnement ? Il me semble même que ce premier contact avec un monde aussi nouveau pour eux ne devrait pas être reporté à un stade trop tardif de leur formation juridique. Et puis-je suggérer que la même démarche s'impose aussi en sens inverse ? Mais cela nous conduit directement au problème capital – et combien délicat ! – des méthodes d'enseignement. . .

même des quatre ou cinq années normalement requises pour leur formation de base (dans le cadre de programmes d'échanges du type Erasmus), soit après l'obtention de leur diplôme et au début de leur vie professionnelle, grâce à la multiplication de ce qu'il est devenu courant dans toutes les langues d'appeler des LL.M. (*master of laws*) : car la première approche d'un droit étranger est souvent déterminante pour la suite et il importe de ne pas manquer ce premier rendez-vous. Dans le même sens, une meilleure articulation de l'enseignement avec la recherche devrait permettre à un nombre plus significatif d'étudiants de préparer leur thèse de doctorat dans cette discipline (notamment grâce à la possibilité aujourd'hui accordée d'une co-tutelle avec un collègue d'une Université étrangère) et orienter définitivement vers le droit comparé une part notable de ceux qui sont appelés à devenir eux-mêmes les formateurs de demain. Enfin, il va de soi que tout ce que nous conseillons à nos étudiants d'aller chercher au-delà de nos frontières, nous devons l'offrir de la même façon aux étrangers qui tentent de le trouver chez nous, peut-être en faisant quelques efforts notables au double plan de l'accueil et – surtout – de la pédagogie...

Ces quelques remarques nous amènent justement à un dernier point essentiel, qui est celui de l'internationalisation des études de droit comparé. Car tout ne peut être accompli dans un cadre strictement national et nous sommes dans un domaine où il est important de créer entre les étudiants (voire les professeurs) de tous pays un climat qui soit à la fois de coopération et d'émulation pour obtenir de meilleurs résultats et permettre l'établissement de liens plus durables. Il faut donc encourager, non seulement l'enseignement de la matière à l'échelle internationale (comme c'est déjà la vocation d'institutions diverses, depuis la Faculté internationale de droit comparé de Strasbourg, qui a joué un rôle de pionnier dans ce domaine et a été pendant des décennies une pépinière de comparatistes, jusqu'à tel ou tel de ces établissements de prestige qui ont récemment vu le jour dans un certain nombre de pays et attirent des étudiants de qualité issus des horizons les plus divers), mais aussi la mise en place de programmes résultant d'un accord entre Universités nationales et qui, tout en assurant une formation complète dans deux systèmes de droit, permettent à des étudiants, certes soigneusement sélectionnés, l'obtention simultanée des deux diplômes ouvrant, ici et là, l'accès à la profession juridique – ce qui paraît être la solution idéale. Ces programmes, du type de ceux qui fonctionnent, par exemple, entre l'Université de Paris d'une part, le *King's College* de Londres et les Universités Columbia et Cornell aux Etats-Unis d'autre part, bien que ne portant au sens strict que sur un « droit étranger », ne sont-ils pas l'avenir du « droit comparé » ? De la même manière, en ce qui concerne la recherche, il faut soutenir sans réserve, outre la cotutelle de thèses déjà évoquée, la poursuite de travaux menés en commun dans différents pays (ne mentionnons que pour mémoire la magnifique entreprise de l'*Encyclopédie internationale de droit comparé*) et la publication d'ouvrages collectifs écrits sous une direction unique, la prolifération de réseaux plus ou moins institutionnalisés, la formation d'équipes de recherches comprenant des représentants du plus grand nombre possible de systèmes, l'organisation de colloques internationaux, etc. Toutes ces actions que nous voyons se multiplier aujourd'hui et qui ouvrent la voie à une forme de culture juridique, voire de « doctrine » internationale, même en matière de droit interne, résultent d'une lente évolution des esprits au moins autant que d'une modification des structures existantes – et c'est en cela aussi que la mondialisation constitue pour tous les comparatistes un atout précieux.

On ne saurait pourtant s'en tenir ici à l'aspect strictement universitaire et il faut souligner le rôle déterminant que jouent en la matière un certain nombre d'organismes, nationaux (tels que, en France, la Société de législation comparée ou l'Association Henri Capitant des amis de la culture juridique française, l'une et l'autre ayant d'ailleurs des membres ou des comités locaux à l'étranger) ou internationaux (comme, justement, notre Académie internationale de droit comparé, agissant par ses congrès biennaux et quadriennaux, ou l'Association internationale des sciences juridiques, grâce à ses colloques annuels), qui ont pour but de rapprocher les juristes de tous pays et leur permettre de se retrouver de façon régulière pour débattre de thèmes précis : le fait est d'ailleurs que leurs rencontres attirent au fil des ans un public de plus en plus large au point qu'elles sont devenues, au même titre que les échanges interuniversitaires, un instrument privilégié du développement du droit comparé à l'heure actuelle. Mais il existe aussi bien d'autres signes encourageants avec la multiplication, même à l'échelle nationale et dans la plupart des pays, d'institutions poursuivant un but similaire (et je préfère n'en citer aucune plutôt que d'en omettre une seule) ou de revues consacrées au droit comparé (et qui, aujourd'hui, hésitent de moins en moins à publier en plusieurs langues pour étendre leur audience). Il faut enfin faire une place à l'action exercée par les diverses professions du droit, qui ont parfaitement compris le sens de l'évolution en cours (et il suffit, par exemple, pour s'en rendre compte, de noter l'importance donnée aux droits étrangers dans la formation dispensée en France aux futurs avocats). Pour un juriste de ma génération, c'est presque une révolution qui s'opère sous nos yeux. Comment pourrait-on, dans ces conditions, douter de l'avenir du droit comparé ?

Encore faut-il pour cela que nos futurs comparatistes ne tombent pas dans le piège qui leur est parfois tendu d'un excès de théorisation sur leur discipline, pouvant conduire à une véritable paralysie de la recherche – et c'est sur ce thème que je voudrais maintenant conclure, car il me paraît capital. Même si le droit comparé est devenu une science, il ne faut pas que celle-ci soit purement spéculative, enfermée dans des règles trop strictes ou réservée à quelques gardiens du temple – et je regrette un peu, à cet égard, que le débat sur son avenir porte aujourd'hui presque exclusivement sur des questions de méthode, en soi parfaitement légitimes, mais qui peuvent créer un risque d'enlisement quand elles ne sont pas suffisamment axées sur la pratique. Serait-ce que les comparatistes doutent d'eux-mêmes à ce point - ou qu'ils éprouvent quelque frustration de ne pas être pris pour de vrais philosophes ? Ou s'agit-il simplement d'une de ces « maladies infantiles » qui affectent toute science nouvelle ? Pour ma part, et à l'instar d'André Tunc, qui reconnaissait volontiers avoir « travaillé les droits étrangers au ras du sol »[7], mais nous a laissé une œuvre impressionnante, je tends à me satisfaire d'une démarche assez empirique

[7]Tunc (1995), VII. – Il faut lire aussi dans cet ouvrage les «Conclusions» de Vanderlinden (1995) auxquelles je souscris sans réserve.

et pragmatique. Car le constat s'impose : pendant que quelques initiés se perdent dans des discussions stériles, au risque de sombrer parfois dans la critique systématique ou le verbalisme, la véritable comparaison tend un peu à stagner et, si notre discipline persévère dans cette voie, elle se privera de bien des concours qui pourraient lui être précieux. J'ai la faiblesse de penser que, dans ce domaine comme en bien d'autres, la vraie méthode s'apprend sur le terrain – et que, d'ailleurs, il y a non pas *une*, mais *des* méthodes en droit comparé, qui varient aussi bien avec le but ou l'objet de la recherche (suivant la matière ou le système juridique choisi) qu'avec la personnalité de chacun, de sorte que, suivant le mot de Jacques Vanderlinden, « il y a autant de manières de comparer les droits qu'il y a de comparatistes ». Or ce pluralisme méthodologique me paraît être une source de richesse, même s'il n'en résulte pas, loin de là, que tout soit permis, car il faut évidemment se garder de la moindre facilité qui pourrait conduire à des analyses superficielles ou des conclusions erronées : mais je crois qu'il n'y a pas plus en la matière de véritable orthodoxie qu'il ne doit y avoir d'anathème et que les premières qualités requises d'un comparatiste sont celles d'un esprit curieux et perspicace, ouvert sur le monde et tolérant, exigeant envers soi-même, mais par-dessus tout doté de ce sens du relatif qui est une forme de la modestie. Voilà la voie à suivre et le reste sera donné par surcroît.

Aussi bien n'est-il pas certain que le droit comparé de demain doive être très différent de celui que nous connaissons aujourd'hui. Je souhaite simplement qu'il se situe dans son prolongement, tout en cherchant, bien sûr, à progresser sans cesse, mais sans marquer de véritable rupture. Je ne perçois, en l'état, pas plus la nécessité que la possibilité même de « comparer autrement ». Et c'est déjà là, pour moi, une raison suffisante d'espérer...

Références

Kischel VU (2016) La méthode en droit comparé – L'approche contextuelle. Revue internationale de droit comparé 907–926

Legrand P (1999) Le droit comparé. PUF, Paris

Markesinis VB (2003) Comparative law in the courtroom and classroom. Hart, Oxford

Sacco R (1991) La comparaison juridique au service de la connaissance du droit. Economica, Paris

Tunc A (1995) Libre propos. In: Vanderlinden J (ed) Comparer les droits, Belgique, Kluwer et E. Story-Scientia, coll. A la rencontre du droit, p VII

Vanderlinden J (1995) Conclusions. In: Vanderlinden J (ed) Comparer les droits, Belgique, Kluwer et E.Story-Scientia, coll. A la rencontre du droit, pp 397–428

Coopération internationale scientifique et tradition de la culture juridique française

Attila Harmathy

1. Comment peut-on esquisser l'activité de quelqu'un ? Il me semble qu'une des possibilités est d'étudier l'activité de la personne concernée et chercher les éléments caractéristiques. Après avoir étudié une partie des publications du professeur Blanc-Jouvan je pense qu'il y a deux remarques qui reflètent des aspects importants de son activité pendant sa carrière.

En 2000 professeur Blanc-Jouvan, directeur-rédacteur en chef de la Revue internationale de droit comparé, président de la Société de législation comparé, expert et puis président de l'Association internationale des sciences juridiques, trésorier de l'Académie internationale de droit comparé – résumant les problèmes du droit comparé au commencement du XXIe siècle – soulignait l'importance de la collaboration des comparatistes de tous les pays[1].

En 1979 professeur Blanc-Jouvan, le nouveau secrétaire générale de la Société de législation comparée exprimait la reconnaissance à son prédécesseur et constatait comme résultat important « le rayonnement de la culture juridique française et l'expansion des études comparatives »[2].

Référence est faite à ces phrases car il me semble que les constatations reflètent le point de vue de Blanc-Jouvan, ce qu'il a considéré l'élément essentiel de l'activité de la Société et l'objectif à atteindre par son activité personnel professionnel aussi. Si l'on veut comprendre quelle sorte de l'activité est requise pour servir la réalisation de cet objectif, on comprend que la tâche est immense: elle englobe en même temps des

[1]Blanc-Jouvan (2000), p. 15.

[2]Blanc-Jouvan (1979), p. 146.

A. Harmathy (✉)
Faculty of Law Eötvös Loránd University, Budapest, Hungary
e-mail: harmathy@ajk.elte.hu

K. Boele-Woelki, D. P. Fernàndez Arroyo (eds.), *The Past, Present and Future of Comparative Law - Le passé, le présent et le futur du droit comparé*, Ius Comparatum – Global Studies in Comparative Law 29, https://doi.org/10.1007/978-3-319-93770-0_8

activités organisatrices et diplomatiques, recherche scientifique et enseignement. Un élément essentiel est requis aussi : on doit avoir une personnalité qui peut construire et maintenir une équipe d' assistant(e)s. Pour mieux comprendre les tâches et les possibilités de la réalisation des objectifs, on doit prendre en connaissance les circonstances, les données de réalisation des activités souhaitées. Le rapport court essaye à faire une esquisse de ces activités faisant allusion aux facteurs historiques, scientifiques, politiques.

2. Le cinquantenaire de la Revue internationale de droit comparé a rendu l'occasion de marquer l'anniversaire du Congrès international de droit comparé qui se tint à Paris en 1900 et qui – selon la formulation de Blanc-Jouvan – a un peu constitué la naissance du droit comparé à l'époque moderne[3].

L'intérêt agrandi au droit comparé au commencement du XXème siècle n'était pas sans antécédents. Pendant la deuxième partie du XIXème siècle il y avait des changements importants dans le domaine de l'économie, dans la société, dans le rôle de l'état, dans la vie politique. Le rôle du commerce international, l'intégration des marchés s'est agrandie, une sorte de globalisation se développait[4]. Le rôle des villes s'est agrandi, les tâches de l'administration publique sont changées, l'importance de la législation est devenue plus importante[5]. Ces événements pouvaient avoir un rôle dans la fondation de la Société de législation comparée, puis de l'organisation d'un comité de législation comparée dans le cadre du Ministère de justice en France et quelques années plus tard dans la création de l'*English Society of Comparative Legislation* au Royaume Uni[6]. L'intérêt envers de la comparaison se présentait dans les états allemands aussi, mais les tendances étaient différentes de celles mentionnées. Un intérêt fort se présentait envers ethnologie et les sciences linguistiques et d'autre part envers les différentes sortes de l'activité de l'État. Les recherches dans le domaine de l'ethnologie juridique étaient influencées par l'activité de Josef Kohler et dans le domaine publiciste par Lorenz von Stein.[7] L'activité de Kohler, qui avait une importance particulière se concentrait d'ailleurs sur l'activité de l'esprit et la culture (chez les tribus primitives et les populations des pays développés également)[8]. Dans le domaine du droit civil les travaux préparatoires étaient au centre sans un intérêt particulier aux analyses comparatives. Le développement de l'économie, la demande d'étudier et d'élaborer des règles nouvelles dans le domaine des sociétés, des actions ont éveillé un intérêt envers les solutions étrangères. Par conséquent c'étaient des jeunes économistes et juristes (influencés par l'activité de Kohler, Schmoller, Wagner) qui ont initié en 1893 d'établir une société de la théorie juridique et économique comparative[9],

[3]Blanc-Jouvan (1999), p. 748.

[4]Broadberry and O'Rourke (2010), II. 6–9.

[5]Bell (2007), pp. 293–294.

[6]Rheinstein (1968), IX. 206.

[7]Kaden (1938), VI. 14, 26–27.

[8]Kohler in: von Holtzendorff and Kohler (1904), pp. 14–15.

[9]Buxbaum (1996), p. 208.

La France avait un rôle particulièrement important de point de vue du droit comparé. N'oubliant pas les changements démographiques, sociaux, le développement de l'économie et les changements politiques semblent avoir une importance particulière. Le rôle du parlement et de la législation devenait plus important et il y avait des changements dans l'enseignement universitaire aussi. L'enseignement de l'histoire du droit, de l'économie politique, de législation industrielle ou coloniale était introduit, et un nombre des juristes avait intérêt à la sociologie (Comte, Durkheim, Tarde), en général aux sciences sociales[10]. Les changements importants mentionnés, l'activité de la Société de législation comparé (depuis 1869), la publication de l'Annuaire de législation étrangère (dépuis 1872) ont contribué à l'établissement de la base d'organisation du premier Congrès international de droit comparé qui avait lieu en 1900 à Paris[11]. Lambert a formulé la raison de l'organisation du Congrès : la Société française de droit comparé a pris conscience de l'incertitude et de la diversité des opinions sur le rôle du droit civil comparé et elle a provoqué l'organisation d'un congrès international à Paris[12]. Lambert a souligné d'une part l'importance pratique de la comparaison (information pour le législateur des mérites et des défauts, des résultats économiques et sociaux des réglementations étrangères), d'autre part la reconnaissance de deux disciplines distinctes : une science sociale (une partie de la sociologie) et une discipline juridique (création et application du droit)[13].

3. La guerre mondiale a mis fin temporairement à la coopération internationale. L'espoir de la recherche libre, des rapports culturels et scientifiques a survécu à la guerre et aux conséquences politiques. Une série des institutions internationales étaient établies qui assuraient la possibilité de la coopération dans le domaine du droit comparé aussi. Des exemples particulièrement importants étaient l'UNIDROIT et l'Académie internationale de droit comparé.

L'Académie internationale de droit comparé a été fondé en 1924 sous l'égide de la Société des Nations. Selon les statuts l'objet principal de l'Académie est de travailler à l'étude du droit comparé sur la base historique et à l'amélioration de la législation dans les divers pays – particulièrement en matière de droit privé – par le rapprochement systématique et la conciliation des lois. Au commencement il n'y avait que trente membres (professeurs d'université)[14].

L'enseignement du droit comparé n'est pas disparu aux universités et il faut mentionner l'établissement en 1926 d'un institut de recherche de droit comparé dans le domaine du droit civil et commercial en Allemagne ayant une importance internationale jusqu'à nos jours. Les circonstances politiques de l'époque peuvent

[10]Halperin (1996), pp. 171–173, 177–178.

[11]Fauvarque-Cosson (2011), pp. 528–530.

[12]Lambert (1903), I.9.

[13]Lambert (1903), I.45, 103, 912–916.

[14]Balogh (1928), pp. 3–7, 14–17. On peut observer qu'un civiliste, comparatiste excellent: professeur Rabel ne pouvait participer qu'après plusieurs ans.

être caractérisées par le fait que le fondateur, Ernst Rabel indiquait l'importance d'un institut de recherche de droit comparé disant que l'institut chercherait l'interprétation des règles juridiques des Alliés[15]. L'importance de cette argumentation peut être compris si l'on prend en considération une remarque faite par Gutteridge qui a souligné l'importance de la coopération internationale juridique et constatait : « Les dangers consécutifs à une politique d'isolement juridique ont été illustrés de façon frappante par les désillusions des juristes allemands lorsqu'ils durent constater que le Traité de Versailles n'allait pas être interprété, ainsi, qu'ils avaient un peu naïvement supposé ... »[16]. La recherche comparative était alors au centre de l'activité de l'Académie, mais l'enseignement n'était pas oublié non plus. L'étude de Lambert portait – entre autres – sur le besoin d'une faculté internationale de droit[17].

La situation politique en Europe n'a pas permis la continuation de la coopération parmi les membres de l'Académie (et en générale des peuples) et après le congrès à la Haye en 1937 l'Académie n'avait pas la possibilité de continuer son activité. Le recommencement des travaux avait lieu en 1950 mais les conditions ont changés et il ne s'agissait plus de l'élaboration des codes uniformes. L'Académie favorise néanmoins la recherche en droit comparé et contribue au développement des rapports entre les peuples. Des congrès internationaux ont été de nouveau organisés tous les quatre ans depuis 1950[18].

La date de recommencement de l'activité de l'Académie est importante. L'an 1950 faisait partie de la période de guerre froide. Quand quelque sorte de coopération entre les juristes des pays des blocs opposés pouvait être envisagée, cela avait une importance particulière. Mais on peut observer d' autres essais d'établissement de rapports entre les deux blocs des pays par l'intermédiaire du droit dans le cadre de l'UNESCO. En 1950 a été constitué le Comité international de droit comparé (depuis 1955 nommé l'Association internationale des sciences juridiques) fonctionnant sous les auspices de l'UNESCO[19]. L'activité de l'UNESCO et de l'Académie était de plus en plus importante de point de vue d'un autre changement important global : les colonies devenaient libres. Dans le domaine du droit comparé un processus lent commençait.

Un domaine de la détente était l'enseignement du droit comparé. Felipe de Solà y Canizares et sa femme ont réussi à établir la Faculté internationale pour l'enseignement de droit comparé à Strasbourg avec le soutien de la France. La Faculté avait chaque année une session de printemps à Strasbourg et une session d'été dans différentes villes depuis 1961. Canizares était secrétaire général de l'Académie internationale de droit comparé aussi depuis 1958 et pouvait établir des rapports avec les juristes de l'Amérique latine et les juristes du bloc soviétique

[15]Buxbaum (1996), pp. 208–209.

[16]Gutteridge (1938), I. 297.

[17]É. Lambert, « Le droit commun de la Société des Nations, Ses organes actuels, Ses organes à venir, Le besoin d'une Faculté internationale de droit », Balogh (1928), 126 et suiv.

[18]Fernandez Arroyo (2015), pp. 13–15.

[19]Blanc-Jouvan (2007), pp. 4–8.

aussi[20]. En conséquence des professeurs russes et ceux des pays socialistes de l'Europe central et oriental participaient régulièrement aux congrès de l'Académie et aux sessions de la Faculté également. Ces rapports avaient des résultats important dans les changements des années 1980 et 1990. Un élément important de coopération était aussi la préparation de l'International Encyclopedia of Comparative Law organisée par le Max-Planck-Institut für ausländisches und internationales Privatrecht, Hamburg.

C'étaient les années 1960 quand l'activité de Blanc-Jouvan déployait. Il faisait des études postgraduelles à Cornell University (Etats-Unis). Le Prix du Centre français de droit comparé a été attribué à lui pour sa thèse en 1957. Il était professeur à Madagascar, puis à Aix-en-Provence et depuis 1969 à la Faculté de Droit de Paris (Université Paris I). Depuis les années 1960 il enseignait à la Faculté internationale de droit comparé aussi. (Une remarque personnelle : moi aussi, comme un chercheur de l'Institut juridique de l'Académie de Sciences de Hongrie, j'ai reçu la permission de faire des études à la Faculté et c'était à Lisbonne en 1964 que j'ai rencontré Professeur Blanc-Jouvan et son épouse pour la première fois à l'occasion de la session d'été de la Faculté).

4. La Revue internationale de droit comparé jouait un rôle important dans la vie scientifique française et internationale. La Revue avait un prédécesseur qui existait depuis la fondation de la Société de législation comparée en 1869. Au commencement le Bulletin de la Société n'a visé qu'à renseigner les membres de l'activité de l'Association. Au XXe siècle le caractère s'était transformé et des études des juristes étrangers étaient publiées aussi. Après la deuxième guerre mondiale on voulait aller plus loin et on voulait assurer que tous les juristes de toutes les branches du droit puissent avoir la possibilité de publication. L'ambition était d'avoir une revue où ils peuvent trouver des études consacrées à l'évolution des grands problèmes de droit dans les différents systèmes de droit qui se partagent le monde[21]. 25 ans plus tard le directeur-rédacteur en chef de la Revue à ce temps, Marc Ancel présentait brièvement un compte rendu de l'activité de cette période. Il a accentué que d'une manière pionnière la Revue s'est lancée dans une entreprise nouvelle après la guerre mondiale et inaugurait une forme nouvelle des relations internationales : les journées juridiques bilatérales. La particularité des journées se présentait d'une part dans la forme nouvelle de coopération internationale, d'autre part dans le choix du partenaire : les deux premières journées avaient lieu entre des juristes français d'une part et des juristes des pays de l'Amérique latine. Le changement du point de départ (traditionnellement la confrontation des droits romanistes et du système de common law) est devenu important parce que l'approche nouvelle pouvait ouvrir le chemin vers les entretiens avec les juristes du bloc soviétiques et plus tard avec ceux du Tiers-Monde[22].

---

[20]David (1965), pp. 572–577.

[21]Avertissement, Revue internationale de droit comparé 1949, 3–5.

[22]Ancel (1975), pp. 5–7.

En 1975 Blanc-Jouvan était déjà rédacteur de la Revue (ensemble avec André Tunc). Il voyait clairement que la Revue avait un rôle capital dans le développement des études comparatives. Selon son opinion il fallait qu'une publication internationale intéressant le droit comparé soit l'œuvre commune des juristes provenant de tous horizon et représentant toutes les grandes familles de droit. Il formulait l'exigence selon laquelle le droit comparé doit contribuer au renforcement des liens entre les juristes des différentes pays et il doit permettre une meilleure compréhension entre les peuples[23].

5. Les tâches se sont poursuivies. Pendant plusieurs années Blanc-Jouvan était président de la Société de législation comparée, Directeur-Rédacteur en chef de la Revue internationale de droit comparé, participait d'une manière continuelle dans les travaux de l'Association internationale des sciences juridiques (pendant trois ans il était président), directeur d'une double maîtrise entre Paris I et King's College, London et il était professeur et chercheur des problèmes juridiques en particulier dans le domaine du droit comparé.

Si quelqu'un a des positions importantes, il peut avoir une influence sur les activités des institutions concernées. On peut essayer de trouver des traces de l'activité à travers des activités des institutions. Des éléments de l'influence peuvent être devinés en étudiant la Revue prenant en considération des circonstances historiques, sociales, économiques.

À l'époque du congrès de 1900 la diversité et l'incertitude des opinions sur la conception et le rôle du droit comparé prévalait[24] et en même temps la nécessité de la coopération internationale économique et politique se faisaient sentir. En 1950 René David constatait : « Sans avoir été à proprement parler, sur le plan académique, l'élève d'Édouard Lambert, je me suis senti constamment en pleine communion d'idées avec lui ». Il a souligné aussi que l'étude des droits étrangers, même si elle peut servir des intérêts très divers, est nécessaire dans le monde nouveau, le droit comparé est un moyen d'acquérir l'esprit international[25]. Blanc-Jouvan, rédacteur-en-chef a continué de poursuivre l'activité dans le domaine de l'édition de la Revue en 1949 et de réaliser les idées exprimées en 1975. Ces mêmes idées servaient comme base dans son activité du secrétaire général, puis président de la Société de législation comparée et comme directeur des travaux scientifiques, puis président de l'Association des sciences juridiques, également comme membre du Bureau de l'Académie internationale de droit comparé.

Un terrain de l'activité – ce qu'on pourrait qualifier diplomatie culturelle – était (et restait jusqu'à nos jours) l'organisation des journées juridiques bi- ou bien multilatérales. On peut penser que les rapports avec les pays du « bloc soviétique » ont été mis au premier plan jusqu'aux années de 1990. Tout d'abord la participation dans la détente, plus tard une sorte de l'éducation des partenaires, la transmission des résultats de la culture juridique et politique de l'Ouest et en particulier ceux de la

[23]Blanc-Jouvan (1975), pp. 57–58, 65.
[24]Lambert (1903), pp. 9–11.
[25]David (1950a), II, VI.

France avaient une importance. De l'autre côté il était important aussi de faire connaitre le système communiste et la Revue publiait des articles sur quelques éléments du droit des états concernés.

Une de ces journées avait lieu en Hongrie – par chance – à une période importante. Une délégation française (présidée par Blanc-Jouvan) a séjourné à Budapest quand l'enterrement, deuxième, cette fois solennelle du premier-ministre et quelques autres leaders de la révolution hongroise de 1956, exécutés après l'intervention de l'armée soviétique, avait lieu. Cet événement est devenu une de masse manifestation et il est considéré comme un pas important dans le cadre du processus de la chute du régime. Les membres de la délégation française avaient la chance d'observer les événements historiques.

La disparition de l'Union soviétique, les éléments de la construction des systèmes nouveaux dans une série des états se présentaient comme des phénomènes historiques, politiques, juridiques, économiques et sociaux. Les éléments du processus ont été présentés par la Revue. Étudiant la Revue le lecteur peut recevoir des informations concernant des acteurs et des problèmes de la transformation de grande importance. La Revue et ses rédacteurs étaient acteurs et chroniqueurs du processus.

Tenant compte du caractère, des conditions financières, personnelles, linguistiques il est remarquable que la Revue puisse refléter beaucoup des changements importants historiques. Des informations et des articles étaient publiés sur les changements juridiques dans le tiers monde aussi. Les questions juridiques des États d'Afrique et d'Asie se présentaient plus souvent depuis les années 1980. Les journées juridiques franco-chinoises, franco-japonaises se sont multipliées. Les problèmes d' harmonisation et d' unification des règles juridiques à l'échelle internationale, dans le domaine de l'Union européenne, dans les relations des pays africaines étaient présentés de plus en plus souvent. Il n'est pas par hasard que Bénédicte Fauvarque-Cosson a qualifié Blanc-Jouvan « ambassadeur de la France et du droit français »[26].

6. Les thèmes juridiques scientifiques discutés ont aussi un intérêt évaluant la rédaction. L'aperçu superficiel du contenu de la Revue de derniers quarante ans montre que la liste des thèmes discutés par les articles publiés est riche. Il est évident que ce sont les études sur différentes problèmes du droit comparé qui sont au centre de l'intérêt de la Revue. Les représentants des conceptions différentes ont eu la possibilité de publier leurs idées. Les questions de l'enseignement du droit comparé (y compris l'enseignement du droit national aux étudiants étrangers et l'enseignement du droit étranger aux étudiants nationaux) étaient discutées plusieurs fois aussi.

Le domaine principal des articles est le droit civil. En comparaison avec plusieurs pays le droit civil est considéré d'une manière large est le droit de famille est y compris. Prenant en considération les transformations des familles pendant et après la deuxième guerre mondiale, les différences sociales entre les pays de l'Est et

[26]Fauvarque-Cosson (2016), p. 281.

l'Ouest, la globalisation, les problèmes appartenant au domaine de droit de famille sont parmi les plus importants questions sociales[27]. En conséquence de la transformation de l'économie et de la société, le domaine du droit de travail est devenu un des domaines les plus intéressants pour les citoyens et pour les entrepreneurs, pour les sociétés également. Les conceptions de faire valoir les droits, les systèmes judiciaires, le fonctionnement des cours se présentaient assez souvent parmi les études publiées dans la Revue. Par rapport avec les transformations politiques les institutions, les règles et les conceptions du droit publiques se sont situées au centre d'intérêt et par conséquent les études portant sur ces questions étaient publiées dans la Revue assez souvent (par exemple le rôle et le fonctionnement des cours constitutionnelles).

La sensibilité de la rédaction de la Revue se présente dans le domaine de la publication des études portant sur les phénomènes nouveaux. Quelques exemples (indiquant la date de la parution de l'article) : protection des données personnelles (1987), informatique (1991), biotechnologie (1992), recherche génétique, euthanasie (2006). Ce n'était pas une exception que la Revue publiait des articles sur les lois nouvelles de grande importance; par exemple l'indemnisation des victimes d'accidents de la circulation (1989, 1992), établissement d'une Cour constitutionnelle (1990).

Un élément essentiel de la Revue est la bibliographie. Les publications des différents pays peuvent servir les chercheurs et les praticiens également. Les comptes rendus et la liste des livres, l'information concernant des revues nouvelles sont très importants. On peut imaginer que la continuité de ce service requiert un réseau des juristes qui rend des informations et des collaborateurs parlant des langues des publications des différents pays. Le maintien de la continuité et la richesse de cette information est le résultat de la rédaction soigneuse.

7. Le droit comparé avait toujours un rôle décisif dans l'activité professionnelle de Blanc-Jouvan. Cette caractéristique se présentait d'une manière différente dans ses publications. Les questions concernant l'essence du droit comparé n'étaient pas au centre de l'analyse dans l'étude sur les droits fonciers collectifs dans les coutumes malgaches[28]. Tout de même la conception du droit comparé, l'analyse d'un système en sa complexité, prenant en considération l'histoire, les traditions familiales, la conception du droit de propriété, la manière des transactions, la pratique administrative sont présentées. L'étude reflète clairement la conception de l'auteur concernant le droit comparé. Dans quelques autres articles qui portent sur le droit français on trouve l'analyse d'une manière éloignée, l'analyse d'une partie d'un système juridique, économique et sociale, ce qui permet la comparaison avec d' autres systèmes[29]. Ces travaux expriment en même temps la sensibilité sociale de l'auteur.

---

[27]Kaelble (2007), pp. 412–417.

[28]Blanc-Jouvan (1964), pp. 333–368.

[29]Blanc-Jouvan (1990), pp. 693–724, et le rapport présenté au Xème Congrès international de Droit Comparé en 1978 à Budapest: Le problème des licenciements collectifs en droit français.

8. C'était tout de même le droit comparé qui était le centre d'intérêt principal. La conception du droit comparé n'était pas généralement acceptée dès le commencement du développement au XIXème siècle. Les interprétations différentes se présentaient non seulement à l'échelle de la définition mais concernant le rôle du droit comparé aussi. La richesse des prises de positions concernant le droit comparé est connue, tout de même il ne semble pas superflu de mentionner quelques idées typiques à fin d'éclaircir la situation et la position de Blanc-Jouvan.

Le point de départ peut être servi par Lambert. Il distinguait deux disciplines sous la dénomination du droit comparé. La première est une science spéculative qui fait partie de la sociologie juridique, tandis que l'autre poursuit un but pratique servant comme un des instruments de la législation ou de l'application du droit[30]. Une autre conception d'influence considérable (de Kohler) soulignait le miroitement de l'esprit et de culture d'un peuple, d'une société, de sa pensée[31]. Une approche tout à fait différente considère le droit comparé comme une méthode de travail sans le caractère d'une science[32]. Au contraire, Rheinstein soulignait le caractère scientifique de la comparaison de droit et distinguait deux sortes de comparaison. Si l'on fait une micro-comparaison on étudie un problème dans son contexte social et cherche les possibilités de résoudre le problème. Au cas de la macro-comparaison le système juridique d'une nation est analysé ainsi que les facteurs déterminants[33].

Lors du congrès international de droit comparé en 1900 l'aspect pratique ainsi que la conception scientifique se présentaient. Il était accepté que la tâche du droit comparé était de chercher la solution idéale dans les législations différentes tenant compte des résultats, de l'état économique et social. En même temps il était souligné que la base était d'étudier les faits (dans la sociologie) et rechercher les lois du développement social (dans l'histoire comparative des institutions)[34].

Les événements du congrès de 1900 ne peuvent pas être étudiés d'une manière isolée sans prendre connaissance les circonstances historiques, économiques, politiques. Les changements depuis la deuxième guerre mondiale doivent être considérés dans leur contexte. Pendant les décennies après 1945, devant l'imminence du danger de emploi de la bombe atomique, des méthodes nouvelles étaient exigées. On sent l'atmosphère de cette période lisant les mots du traité de René David publié en 1950 : dans le monde actuel c'est un devoir impérieux de faire un effort pour connaître les pays étrangers, comprendre leur manière de voir. Et il a ajouté que si l'on dépasse le stade de l'étude des droits étrangers, et que l'on passe à la comparaison proprement dite des droits, celle-ci, à son tour, va pouvoir servir des intérêts très divers, le principal de ces intérêts est d'élever le droit à la hauteur d'une véritable science[35]. Plus tard les exigences de la globalisation, l'intégration,

---

[30]Lambert (1903), pp. 915–916.

[31]Kohler in: von Holtzendorff and Kohler (1904), p. 15.

[32]Kaden (1938), pp. 9, 11.

[33]Rheinstein (1968), p. 208.

[34]Arminjon et al. (1950), I. 176–177.

[35]David (1950a), II.

l'unification des règles avaient de plus en plus d'importance. Tout de même on ne peut pas oublier l'observation de Sacco que les essais à justifier le droit comparé se référant aux emplois pratiques peuvent être ridicules; la tâche du droit comparé est d'acquérir une meilleure connaissance des institutions juridiques[36]. Étant donné que l'expérimentation n'est pas possible, le droit comparé peut être utilisé à fin d'obtenir une meilleure compréhension des problèmes[37]. Selon la formulation de Zweigert et Kötz l'objectif du droit comparé en est devenu un vrai droit comparé international qui peut servir comme base de la science juridique universelle[38].

Depuis quelques décennies l'intérêt pour le droit comparé a agrandi et des conceptions très diverses ont été élaborées. Sans essayer à donner une vue d'ensemble on peut mentionner qu'il y a une tendance forte de faire usage de la comparaison dans l'espace européen servant l'objectif du développement de l'Union européenne[39]. D'autre part il est remarquable qu'une grande variété des théories portant sur le droit comparé en général, la comparaison dans le domaine des différentes branches de droit, les objectifs variés de l'utilisation de la comparaison sont apparus[40].

Sans essayer d'énumérer les différentes théories il semble nécessaire de mentionner deux points de vue à cause de leurs effets. L'élément commun de ces théories est la considération que la dépendance du droit des facteurs sociaux, culturels, historiques n'a pas une importance décisive. Selon cette conception la transplantation des règles juridiques est un phénomène commun de beaucoup de systèmes juridiques et la méthode de transplanter des règles juridiques est particulièrement avantageuse pour le développement[41]. Dans l'année de la publication de cette théorie un article de Kahn-Freund a été publié qui a expliqué que la transplantation des règles juridiques sans avoir regard à leur contexte social et politique constitue un abus[42].

L'autre point de vue, assez répandu, considère que ce sont les effets économiques des règles juridiques qui ont une importance[43]. Ce point de vue peut avoir des conséquences sérieuses. Suivant cette ligne on peut arriver à la constation que les systèmes juridiques des nations différentes peuvent promouvoir le développement économique de manière différente. Par conséquent si les organisations internationales ou bien banques ont la tâche de promouvoir le développement des pays différents, elles doivent initier l'application d'un système (ou bien les institutions de ce système) qui est le plus efficace. La réaction de la part des juristes français

[36]Sacco (1991), pp. 2–5.

[37]Glendon (1987), p. 1.

[38]Zweigert and Kötz (1998), p. 46.

[39]Michaels (2009), II. 1267–1269.

[40]Reimann and Zimmermann (2008), VIII.

[41]Watson (1974), pp. 95–96.

[42]Kahn-Freund (1974), p. 27.

[43]Ogus (2007), p. 158.

était très négative[44]. Mais le point de vue de l'application de l'approche économique mentionnée a été rejeté sur la base de différentes autres analyses aussi[45].

9. On peut finir le petit essai du tour d'horizon avec les mots de Blanc-Jouvan : Plus que jamais le droit comparé semble être aujourd'hui à la croisée des chemins. D'un côté, sa légitimité est incontestée, mais d'autre côté, il en est résulté une sorte de crise d'identité.

Il faut tenir compte de sa conclusion aussi : Le droit comparé ne pourra progresser que grâce à travail de tous et il pourra servir de base d'une nouvelle science juridique universelle[46].

10. Les conceptions du droit comparé, et l'activité de Blanc-Jouvan aussi sont étroitement liées avec l'enseignement du droit comparé. Dans ce domaine il y a un assez grand nombre de conceptions différentes.

En 1950 René David expliquait que les universités françaises ne négligent pas l'intérêt pratique qui s'attache à la connaissance des droits étrangers, mais elles donnent à l'enseignement du droit comparé un aspect plus théorique. Les études de droit comparé ont été conçues avant tout à élargir les vues, à mieux comprendre l'évolution du droit, développer la culture juridique[47]. Quelque décennie plus tard, Blanc-Jouvan continue le discours avec les mêmes idées. Pendant la période depuis 1950 l'importance du droit comparé a été admise, mais même les questions de départ n'ont pas été éclairées. Une de ces questions était à ce temps aussi le profil de l'enseignement juridique universitaire (à quoi sert l'enseignement : directement la pratique ou bien une formation plus générale, quel est le rôle de la spécialisation, etc.). Une autre question fondamentale restait non-résolue la méthode de l'enseignement du droit comparé (ici aussi la question se pose: manière dogmatique ou pratique). Naturellement il y a des problèmes fondamentaux : l'infrastructure de l'enseignement, cest d' dire la bibliothèque contenant les livres et revues étrangères servant la base de l'enseignement. Même le contenu de l'enseignement n'est pas fixé. On doit préciser aussi au commencement quelle est la base de référence, car la traduction simple de la dénomination des institutions juridiques étrangères n'est pas suffisante. Une introduction globale semble nécessaire avant qu'on puisse étudier les institutions juridiques spécifiques. Il faut spécifier le système juridique, et les institutions de ce système enseigné tenant compte en même temps des changements de son propre système juridique. La logique du système nous conduit à une autre série des problèmes commençant par la formation des futurs enseignants. Le système des rapports internationaux est aussi une condition nécessaire de l'éducation. La conclusion convainquante de l'étude de Blanc-Jouvan est que l'Université doit prendre ses responsabilités, le temps de l'amateurisme est fini[48].

---

[44]Fauvarque-Cosson and Kerhuel (2009), pp. 811–829.

[45]Par exemple Siems and Deakin (2010), pp. 124–128; Pistor (2010), pp. 352–359.

[46]Blanc-Jouvan (2000), pp. 8, 15.

[47]David (1950b), pp. 682–683.

[48]Blanc-Jouvan (1996), pp. 347–367.

L'enseignement du droit comparé était au centre des intérêts de Blanc-Jouvan pendant toute son activité et non seulement comme professeur mais aussi comme rédacteur en chef de la Revue internationale de droit comparé. Des études portant sur différentes questions de l'enseignement étaient souvent publiées par la Revue[49].

11. À la fin de cet éloge une petite référence doit être faite à une série publiée par la Revue internationale de droit comparé. C'était la série des hommages rendus aux différentes personnalités du droit comparé. Blanc-Jouvan était souvent l'auteur de ces commémorations. Il était touchant de lire les hommages écrits par lui toujours avec beaucoup de soin, d'éloquence, d'amitié et ses écrits ont reflété non seulement la personne de qui il est mais également la personnalité de l'écrivain et sa foi.

Références

Ancel M (1975) Le XXVe anniversaire de la Revue. Revue internationale de droit comparé 5

Arminjon P, Nolde B, Wolf M (1950) Traité de Droit Comparé. LGDJ, Paris

Balogh E (1928) Mémoires de l'Académie Internationale de Droit Comparé. Sack, Sweet and Maxwell, Rivière I

Bell J (2007) Administrative law in a comparative perspective. In: Örücü E, Nelken D (eds) Comparative law. Hart, Oxford, Portland, pp 293–294

Blanc-Jouvan X (1964) Les droits fonciers collectifs dans les coutumes malgaches. Revue Internationale de droit comparé 333

Blanc-Jouvan X (1975) Le rôle international d'une revue de droit comparé. Revue internationale de droit comparé 57

Blanc-Jouvan X (1979) Activité de la Société de Législation Comparée pendant l'année 1978. Revue Internationale de Droit Comparé 146

Blanc-Jouvan X (1990) La flexibilité du temps de travail. Revue Internationale de droit comparé 693

Blanc-Jouvan X (1996) Le point de vue d'un universitaire. Revue Internationale de droit comparé 347

Blanc-Jouvan X (1999) Le cinquantenaire de la Revue. Revue Internationale de Droit Comparé 748

Blanc-Jouvan X (2000) L'Avenir du droit comparé. Société de Législation Comparé, Paris

Blanc-Jouvan X (2007) Association Internationale des Sciences Juridiques à l'aube d'un nouveau millénaire. Association des Sciences Juridique, UNESCO, Paris

Broadberry S, O'Rourke KH (2010) The Cambridge economic history of modern Europe. Cambridge University Press, Cambridge

Buxbaum RM (1996) Die Rechtsvergleichung zwischen nationalem Staat und internationalen Wirtschaft. Rabels Zeitschrift für ausländisches und internationales Privatrecht 208

David R (1950a) Traité élémentaire de droit civil comparé. L.G.D.J., Paris

David R (1950b) Le droit comparé, enseignement de culture générale. Revue Internationale de droit comparé 682

David R (1965) Felipe de Solà Canizares (1905–1965). Revue Internationale de Droit Comparé 572

Fauvarque-Cosson B (2011) Deux siècles d'évolution du droit comparé. Revue Internationale de Droit Comparé 528

Fauvarque-Cosson B (2016) Hommage à Xavier Blanc-Jouvan, directeur de la RIDC. Revue internationale de droit comparé 281

[49]Par exemple en 1988, 1993, 1996, 2002.

Fauvarque-Cosson B, Kerhuel AJ (2009) Is law an economic contest? French reactions to the doing business World Bank reports and economic analysis of the law. Am J Comp Law 811
Fernandez Arroyo D (2015) Annuaire de l'Académie, 9e éd. Académie internationale de droit comparé, Paris
Glendon MA (1987) Abortion and divorce in western law. Harvard U. P., Cambridge, MA, London
Gutteridge HC (1938) La valeur du droit comparé, Introduction à l'étude du droit comparé, Recueil d'études en l'honneur d'Édouard Lambert. Sirey, L.G.D.J., Paris
Halperin JL (1996) Histoire du droit privé français depuis 1804. Presses Universitaires de France, Paris
Kaden EH (1938) Rechtsvergleichung. In: Schlegelberger F (ed) Rechtsvergleichendes Handwörterbuch, vol VI. Vahlen, Berlin, p 14
Kaelble H (2007) Sozialgeschichte Europas 1945 bis zur Gegenwart. Beck, München
Kahn-Freund O (1974) On uses and misuses of comparative law. Mod Law Rev 27
Lambert É (1903) Études de droit commun ou de droit civil comparé, Introduction, La fonction du droit civil comparé. Giard et Brière, Paris
Michaels R (2009) Rechtsvergleichung. In: Basedow J, Hopt KJ, Zimmermann R (eds) Handwörterbuch des Europäischen Privatrechts. Mohr, Siebeck, Tübingen
Ogus A (2007) The economic approach: competititon between legal systems. In: Örücü E, Nelken D (eds) Comparative law, a handbook. Hart, Oxford, Portland
Pistor K (2010) Statistische Rechtsvergleichung, Eine kritische Bestandsaufnahme. Zeitschrift für Vergleichende Rechtswissenschaft 352
Reimann M, Zimmermann R (2008) Preface to the Hardback edition. In: Reimann M, Zimmermann R (eds) The Oxford handbook of comparative law. Oxford UP, Oxford, New York
Rheinstein M (1968) Legal systems. In: Sills DL (ed) International encyclopedia of the social sciences, vol IX. Macmillan, New York
Sacco R (1991) Legal formants: a dynamic approach to comparative law. Am J Comp Law 2
Siems M, Deakin S (2010) Comparative law and finance, past, present and future research. J Inst Theor Econ 124
Von Holtzendorff F, Kohler J (1904) Enzyclopädie der Rechtswissenschaft. Duncker und Humblot, Guttentag, Leipzig, Berlin
Watson A (1974) Legal transplants. Scottish Academic Press, Edinburg
Zweigert K, Kötz HD (1998) Introduction to comparative law, 3rd edn. Clarendon Press, Oxford

Remerciements/Acknowledgements

Xavier Blanc-Jouvan

Madame le Président, Monsieur le Secrétaire général,
Mesdames, Messieurs,
Chers Collègues et Chers Amis,

Me voici un peu étourdi, tant par l'honneur qui m'est fait que par l'ampleur des remerciements que je dois adresser à tous ceux qui m'ont permis de me trouver à cette place aujourd'hui – et en aussi flatteuse compagnie ! Ces remerciements vont d'abord, bien sûr, à notre Académie, à sa Présidente, à son Bureau et à son Secrétaire général, à qui je tiens à exprimer ma bien vive reconnaissance, ainsi qu'à toutes les personnes présentes et à toute la communauté des comparatistes, dont vous êtes, Mesdames, Messieurs, les éminents représentants. Ils vont aussi au Professeur Attila Harmathy, dont la présence et l'amitié me sont si précieuses et dont les mots trop généreux m'ont infiniment touché. Mais ils s'adressent également à bien d'autres personnes qui m'ont aidé, tout au long de mon itinéraire, et que je n'aurais garde d'oublier ce soir.

Car nous le savons bien: chacun d'entre nous a derrière lui une longue histoire – et c'est le cas même des comparatistes, pour qui l'on peut toujours se demander ce qui, dans leur parcours, les a amenés au droit comparé. Hasard ou vocation ? Je me bornerai, pour ce qui me concerne, à évoquer deux menus faits qui ont été, en réalité, déterminants.

Tout est parti, très modestement, de l'offre qui m'a été faite, alors que je venais tout juste de terminer mon premier cycle universitaire et sans que je l'eusse en rien sollicitée, de poursuivre mes études pendant un an dans une Université américaine de

X. Blanc-Jouvan (✉)
Université de Paris 1 Pantheon-Sorbonne, Paris, France

K. Boele-Woelki, D. P. Fernàndez Arroyo (eds.), *The Past, Present and Future of Comparative Law - Le passé, le présent et le futur du droit comparé*, Ius Comparatum – Global Studies in Comparative Law 29, https://doi.org/10.1007/978-3-319-93770-0_9

mon choix. C'était (vous n'en serez pas surpris !) il y a fort longtemps, peu après la fin du grand conflit mondial, et il faut bien comprendre ce que cela représentait à l'époque pour quelqu'un qui n'avait guère quitté encore son pays natal... L'occasion m'a semblé tellement unique que je n'ai pas envisagé un instant de la refuser : et c'est ainsi que j'ai finalement passé l'année 1953-54 à l'Université Cornell, dans l'Etat de New York – une « année de rêve », qui fut pour moi une mine de découvertes, tant à la *Law School* elle-même, où j'ai rencontré l'un des vrais « grands comparatistes » de ce temps, Rudolf Schlesinger, qu'*extra muros*, dans ce pays que j'ai appris à aimer en le sillonnant dans tous les sens, de Boston à San Diego et de Key West à Seattle, et en pratiquant mon anglais « sur la route », un peu (mais un peu seulement...) à la manière de Jack Kerouac ! Tels furent donc mon premier contact avec la *common law* et ma première expérience en droit comparé. On imagine le profit que j'en ai retiré – et l'on voit déjà à qui s'adressent mes premiers remerciements !

Mais ce n'est pas tout, et le destin m'a encore servi, quelques années plus tard, en me permettant d'obtenir mon premier poste d'enseignement à la toute jeune Université de Madagascar. Ce fut à nouveau une grande chance pour moi, parce que j'ai pu m'initier ainsi aux problèmes juridiques de ce que l'on appelait alors un « pays en voie de développement », en fait un pays en pleine mutation à la veille de son accession à l'indépendance. Pendant près de trois ans, j'ai pu participer au travail de collecte et de rédaction des coutumes en même temps que m'intéresser à quelques problèmes relatifs au droit de la terre et contribuer pour une modeste part à l'élaboration d'une loi proprement malgache sur le mariage – prélude à une entreprise de codification dont je ne suis même pas sûr qu'elle soit achevée à ce jour... Il s'agissait bien, à mon sens, d'une forme, sans doute un peu particulière, mais authentique, de droit comparé, teinté d'anthropologie juridique, qui m'a proprement passionné. Je dois donc, là encore, exprimer ma gratitude à mes nombreux amis malgaches qui m'ont ainsi permis d'acquérir une autre vision du droit et facilité l'accès à une culture bien différente de tout ce que j'avais connu jusque-là !

Je n'en dirai pas plus sur ces premiers pas dans une discipline qui n'a depuis lors jamais cessé de m'occuper tout entier. Je n'ai jamais abandonné les deux voies que je m'étais tracées au départ, sans pour autant négliger d'en ouvrir quelques autres dans l'exercice de mes fonctions d'enseignement – et je ne mentionne ce dernier point que pour souligner tout ce que je dois à mes étudiants, et notamment à mes étudiants américains qui, de Columbia à Tulane ou à UCLA, ont su me faire comprendre – et avec quelle gentillesse ! – dans quel esprit un juriste de « droit civil » devait aborder la *common law* : et je sais gré surtout à ceux de l'Université de Chicago, où j'ai eu le privilège de travailler auprès de ce géant du droit comparé que fut Max Rheinstein, d'avoir assuré mon éducation dans ce domaine beaucoup mieux que n'auraient pu le faire des années passées en bibliothèque. Bien sûr, ces tâches pédagogiques ne m'ont pas empêché de me livrer aussi, au cours des ans, à d'autres activités (recherche, encore un peu de codification, cette fois au Rwanda, animation d'organismes divers, dont la très chère Société de législation comparée...), mais je n'ai jamais oublié que mon port d'attache se trouvait d'abord à l'Université - et c'est bien en faveur des étudiants et aux côtés d'André Tunc que j'ai pu contribuer à monter et faire vivre certains programmes d'échange avec de prestigieuses universités étrangères en vue de former les comparatistes de demain.

Je m'en voudrais enfin de ne pas remercier ici tous les collègues, venus des horizons les plus divers, que j'ai eu la bonne fortune de rencontrer sur mon long chemin et qui m'ont, eux aussi, beaucoup appris. Qui peut douter que les amitiés ainsi nouées de par le monde soient le vrai trésor du comparatiste ? Ces amitiés, elles remontent pour moi à l'époque où j'enseignais à cette magnifique institution que fut en son temps la Faculté internationale de droit comparé de Strasbourg, dont il n'est pas inutile de rappeler le rôle crucial qu'elle a joué, à un moment difficile et grâce au dévouement de quelques-uns, dans l'essor du droit comparé – et dont je garde un souvenir inoubliable. Plus récemment, c'est surtout au sein de notre Académie que j'ai pu entretenir ma flamme comparative, comme dans le cadre de l'Association internationale des sciences juridiques (aux destinées de laquelle quatre d'entre nous, ici présents, ont eu tour à tour l'honneur de présider) – deux organismes irremplaçables dans la mesure où ils assurent cette internationalisation du droit comparé qui est, à mes yeux, la meilleure garantie de son avenir. Ce n'est certes pas un paradoxe que d'ajouter aux principales « familles de droit » chères à René David la grande famille des comparatistes – celle à laquelle je dois tant et à qui j'ai l'honneur de redire aujourd'hui, avec ma profonde gratitude, mon indéfectible attachement.

Partie IV / Part IV
Jean-Louis Baudouin

Quelques brèves réflexions sur l'avenir du droit comparé

Jean-Louis Baudouin

L'avenir du droit comparé est bien évidemment difficile à prévoir dans ces temps changeants, sinon, en tenant compte, de façon rétrospective, de son évolution depuis la fin du XIXe siècle. Ce retour en arrière pourrait permettre de mieux identifier certaines tendances prometteuses pour l'avenir.

À l'origine, avec le premier congrès de droit comparé d'Édouard Lambert au tout début du siècle et la fondation par lui en 1921 du premier Institut de droit comparé en France, à Lyon, avec quelques années plus tôt (en 1869) la création de la Société de législation comparée, le droit comparé restait à cette époque l'apanage d'universitaires et d'intellectuels curieux de savoir comment d'autres pays traitaient certaines questions juridiques. Le droit comparé n'avait, pour ainsi dire, que peu de résonnance et de pénétration dans les sphères législatives et jurisprudentielles. C'était essentiellement une discipline basée sur l'identification et l'appréhension des solutions du droit positif étranger et donc, avant tout, une discipline instructionnelle.

Il convient de se souvenir cependant qu'à cette époque les communications étaient lentes et que le rayonnement universel du droit et de la méthode comparative s'en trouvait donc forcément limité.

Au Québec, où la coexistence des deux systèmes de droit civil et de common law existait depuis le milieu du XIXe siècle, l'usage du droit comparé principalement comme outil de mesure des solutions offertes par les deux systèmes était bel et bien vivant. Cette tendance est d'ailleurs demeurée ferme et s'est même accélérée pour une grande partie du XXe siècle. Le droit civil québécois à l'époque était cependant en état de résistance contre l'influence de la common law. L'utilisation du droit

J.-L. Baudouin (✉)
Faculté de droit de l'Université de Montréal, Avocat-conseil Fasken, Montréal, QC, Canada
e-mail: jbaudouin@fasken.com

K. Boele-Woelki, D. P. Fernàndez Arroyo (eds.), *The Past, Present and Future of Comparative Law - Le passé, le présent et le futur du droit comparé*, Ius Comparatum – Global Studies in Comparative Law 29, https://doi.org/10.1007/978-3-319-93770-0_10

comparé a donc été un des facteurs importants de la survie du droit civil québécois. La référence obligée du système de droit civil était essentiellement aux auteurs et à la doctrine française d'abord, aux exégètes, puis ensuite, aux grands traités de l'époque.

Mon père, fait significatif, lorsqu'il a publié son ouvrage de droit civil en 1953, l'a intitulé *« Le droit civil québécois, modèle vivant de droit comparé »*.

D'une façon globale, ce n'est que petit à petit que l'orientation purement positiviste du droit comparé s'est estompée, et ce, surtout vers le milieu du XXe siècle. C'est en effet à cette époque que l'intérêt des juristes a commencé à se porter également sur la structure juridique des grandes familles de droit et de leurs systèmes. Cette évolution s'est manifestée par la parution d'ouvrages qui, au-delà les solutions ponctuelles de droit positif, recherchaient l'évaluation critique et plus globale des différents systèmes et introduisaient peu à peu une « *macro comparaison* ». Je pense par exemple à l'ouvrage de René David et à la place de plus en plus importante de l'analyse comparatiste théorique dans les revues comme la *Revue internationale de droit comparé* ou beaucoup plus tard, en 1952, dans l'*American Journal of Comparative Law*.

À cette époque, le droit comparé s'affirme alors à la fois dans sa dimension intellectuelle et universitaire, mais aussi dans sa dimension d'outil pratique intéressant pour le juge et le législateur à la recherche d'autres solutions, de regard critique sur son propre droit et enfin, dans sa perspective épistémologique.

Désormais, comme le signalait si justement Madame la Présidente de l'Académie de droit comparé, le droit comparé est à la fois science et méthode. À une comparaison axée sur l'inventaire des solutions du droit positif et à l'identification de la spécificité des différents systèmes juridiques issus des grandes familles du droit, vient s'ajouter une troisième dimension, portant cette fois-ci sur les méthodes d'analyse et les techniques de raisonnement comparées. Le cercle paraît donc maintenant complet.

Trois principaux phénomènes me paraissent susceptibles d'influencer désormais l'évolution du droit comparé et pourraient donc avoir éventuellement, dans l'avenir, une certaine portée.

La première est la facilité d'accès à l'information. De nos jours grâce à l'informatique, il est très facile de s'informer sur l'état du droit dans la très grande majorité des pays, et ce, d'une façon extrêmement rapide. Ce nouvel outil me paraît être particulièrement important et utile pour le législateur et le juge en quête d'une comparaison critique de ses propres solutions avec celles des autres pays.

La seconde est la tendance de plus en plus présente de la recherche d'une possible uniformisation des solutions juridiques, principalement dans les secteurs du droit touchant à l'économie. Les traités internationaux sur la circulation des biens en sont bel exemple, les travaux d'Unidroit à un niveau différent en sont un autre.

Enfin, l'évaluation de la méthode comparative elle-même. Elle sera, je pense, davantage axée vers une connaissance intégrée de la réalité culturelle et économique des pays et donc, de tous les facteurs sociaux qui soutiennent les solutions juridiques. Les problèmes de droit comparé ne s'analyseront plus en vase clos, mais en tenant compte des sources touchant à la réalité sociale, culturelle et économique des pays, et intéresseront donc davantage sociologues, politologues et anthropologues.

Le prophète, dit le dicton, n'est qu'un fou et je me garderai donc bien de vouloir prédire l'avenir. Pourtant, il n'est pas du tout assuré que la tendance à la mondialisation et donc, à l'uniformisation des solutions juridiques que nous connaissons à l'heure actuelle, persiste. Il n'est pas certain qu'un retour des nationalismes ne remettra pas en question l'évolution actuelle du droit comparé vers une certaine globalisation et uniformisation des solutions juridiques et au-delà de celles-ci, des systèmes et des grandes familles.

Le savant, le maître, le créateur de la vie universitaire

Marek Safjan

Il est peu de Professeurs de droit qui influencent aussi intensivement la réalité qui les entoure, le milieu professionnel auquel ils appartiennent et des générations de juristes formées dans les Universités où ils enseignent. Jean-Louis Baudouin est une personnalité exceptionnelle et éminente depuis de nombreuses années. Il impose un certain style de pensée juridique, une méthodologie de recherche dans le domaine du droit et des méthodes d'analyse qui lui sont propres. Il appartient au cercle des personnalités juridiques qui, grâce à leur sensibilité, leur érudition, leur expérience et leur charisme sont aptes à identifier clairement les problèmes les plus importants de notre réalité contemporaine et de susciter le débat public. S'agissant de l'impact exercé par Jean-Louis Baudouin sur le milieu universitaire, le Doyen de la Faculté de droit de l'Université de Montréal, Claude Fabien, a dit autrefois, lorsque la médaille pour le 125ème anniversaire de la Faculté lui a été remise :

> [Jean-Louis Baudouin] se situe à la charnière du passage de ce corps des Professeurs d'un état à un autre, par sa gloire personnelle qui abondamment rejaillit sur ses collègues, par la force de son exemple et par l'enthousiasme qu'il a su, comme maître, communiquer à ses élèves. On pourrait dire qu'il y a le corps professoral AVANT Jean-Louis, PENDANT Jean–Louis et APRES Jean-Louis. Je n'ose trop insister sur cette métaphore, car un autre personnage qui a marqué l'histoire, est mort crucifié à 33 ans. Il ne faudrait pas confondre les initiales (J.C.).

L'exceptionnalité de Jean-Louis Baudouin en tant que juriste – Professeur d'Université – s'explique notamment par l'universalité et la multi-dimensionnalité de son activité en tant qu'inspirateur et animateur de recherches scientifiques dans

M. Safjan (✉)
Université de Varsovie, Warszawa, Poland
e-mail: msaf@curia.europa.eu

K. Boele-Woelki, D. P. Fernàndez Arroyo (eds.), *The Past, Present and Future of Comparative Law - Le passé, le présent et le futur du droit comparé*, Ius Comparatum – Global Studies in Comparative Law 29, https://doi.org/10.1007/978-3-319-93770-0_11

les domaines nouveaux liés directement au développement de notre civilisation. Il représente également un modèle exemplaire de Professeur d'université dans la matière juridique, un point de référence presque impossible à atteindre en termes de qualité d'enseignement universitaire (des foules d'étudiants fascinés par ses cours et par ses écrits prouvent la force attirante de Jean-Louis Baudouin). Enfin, en tant que savant qui, avec une grande virtuosité, utilise des méthodes modernes de recherche, en puisant largement dans des études comparatistes mais aussi dans des sources d'Histoire des institutions ayant un impact sur la compréhension contemporaine du droit. On a même parlé de méthode baudouinienne de recherche en expliquant que c'est «une méthodologie tridimensionnelle: verticale par l'histoire, horizontale par le droit comparé et transversale par la pluridisciplinarité» (Claude Fabien).

Jean-Louis Baudouin vient d'une famille de juristes et ce n'est pas un hasard s'il a dirigé sa carrière professionnelle vers le droit. Dans une interview publiée en 2010 (Droit-INC, Leaders, 23 juin 2010), il a dit à propos de cette transmission familiale:

> Dans mon cas, c'était vraiment de la prédestination! C'est presque génétique en fait: je suis la 12ème génération de juristes de la famille. C'est donc dire que le choix était un peu restreint! [. . .] Quant au Droit, mon père était Professeur de droit, mon grand-père était juge et mon arrière-grand-père était Premier président de la Cour de cassation en France.

Ajoutons que c'est heureux que Jean-Louis Baudouin ait choisi la carrière de juriste et n'ait finalement pas décidé de suivre son inclination à être professeur de planche à voile dans une île du Sud ! Il est également nécessaire de souligner l'influence de Jean-Louis Baudouin sur le processus de codification du Droit civil au Québec et son apport significatif aux travaux de la Commission de réforme du droit du Canada, qui a conduit, en 1984, à l'honorer en tant que premier récipiendaire du Prix d'honneur de la Commission de réforme du droit du Canada et de l'Association canadienne des Professeurs de droit pour sa contribution exceptionnelle à la recherche. Sans risque d'exagération, il est juste de dire que le Code civil du Québec, dans sa rédaction actuelle, constitue un excellent exemple d'une codification du droit privé répondant aux défis soulevés par la civilisation moderne.

Jean-Louis Baudouin exploite ses champs d'activité tel un juriste comprenant parfaitement la réalité qui l'entoure et ayant une vision du droit à la fois capable d'adopter la perspective de dispositions isolées et d'envisager le système juridique dans son entier, tout en respectant le rôle exercé par ce dernier pour atteindre l'objectif principal qui est la justice et la pondération d'intérêts différents, souvent en conflit. Cela s'inscrit dans une parfaite conformité avec son activité prestigieuse ultérieure en tant que juge à la Cour d'appel du Québec de 1989 à 2009.

Dans cette partie de mon intervention, je ne peux que très superficiellement et très sélectivement rappeler les fonctions importantes exercées par le Professeur Jean-Louis Baudouin et les titres honorifiques qu'il a reçus. Ceux-ci constituent une preuve éclatante de sa position exceptionnelle dans les milieux universitaires et juridiques en qualité de Professeur éminent de droit, enseignant universitaire renommé et, enfin, en tant que personnalité ayant eu une influence indiscutable sur la formation du système juridique du Québec.

Mentionnons donc que M. Jean-Louis Baudouin est Docteur honoris causa de sept Universités (en France, en Belgique, au Canada) et qu'il a obtenu le titre de Grand Officier de l'Ordre national du Québec (2012) et d'Officier de l'Ordre du Canada (2015).

Il a exercé différentes fonctions : vice-président de la Commission de réforme du droit du Canada (1976-1979), président de la section québécoise de l'Association Henri Capitant (depuis 1973), vice-président international de l'Institut des droits des pays d'expression française (IDEF), membre de la Société canadienne de bioéthique (depuis 1980), secrétaire fondateur de la Ligue des droits de l'Homme (1966), membre du Conseil des sciences du Canada, sur les nouvelles technologies de reproduction (1983-1986), membre correspondant de l'Académie française des sciences d'outremer etc.

Jean-Louis Baudouin a enseigné en tant que Professeur invité dans les Universités suivantes : Mc Gill, Sherbrooke, Toronto, Lisbonne, Varsovie, Fribourg, Louisiana State, Addis Abeba, Gênes, Tokyo, Paris I Panthéon-Sorbonne, Paris-Est Créteil Val de Marne, Aix-en-Provence, Poitiers.

L'Université de Montréal a été le premier point d'attache universitaire de Jean-Louis Baudouin, où il a commencé sa carrière en 1969 en tant que Professeur agrégé, puis, à partir de 1972, en tant que Professeur titulaire de la Faculté de droit. Il a ensuite continué à enseigner comme Professeur associé tout en étant juge à la Cour d'appel du Québec, le plus haut tribunal du Québec.

Dans un certain sens, le couronnement de son activité à l'Université de Montréal a été le lancement de la Chaire Jean-Louis Baudouin en droit civil, dotée d'un fonds d'un million de dollars, le 11 mai 2006, au Pavillon central de l'Université de Montréal, sous la présidence du Recteur de l'Université et en présence de nombreux dignitaires du monde juridique, scientifique et philanthropique. L'œuvre de Jean-Louis Baudouin et son rayonnement sont un fondement fort pour la perpétuation de celle-ci et le maintien de son influence sur les nouvelles générations d'étudiants et sur les enseignants des Facultés de droit, encouragés à suivre son modèle exemplaire de recherches scientifiques et d'enseignement.

Pour achever cette présentation un peu formelle, bien que très significative et même nécessaire pour comprendre la grandeur et la richesse de la personnalité de Jean-Louis Baudouin, il me reste à ajouter que celui-ci appartient aux auteurs les plus connus parmi les grands Professeurs de culture juridique d'expression française et que sa contribution au développement des sciences juridiques est exceptionnelle, non seulement à cause du nombre d'ouvrages qu'il a écrit, mais surtout en vertu de leur grande qualité et de l'étendue extrêmement diversifiée de ses explorations scientifiques.

Avant de présenter les éléments les plus importants de ses remarquables écrits, illustrant son apport au développement de la pensée juridique et à l'amélioration de la culture juridique générale, je ne peux omettre ici quelques souvenirs plus personnels. Je dois ouvertement reconnaître que, dès mes premiers contacts avec Jean-Louis Baudouin, noués en 1982 quand j'ai été Professeur invité à l'Université de Montréal, je suis devenu un grand admirateur de son style, de sa manière d'exercer son activité universitaire aussi bien dans le domaine de l'enseignement que de la recherche. J'étais, à cette époque, un peu perdu dans la nouvelle réalité canadienne, étant citoyen d'un État, la Pologne, dans lequel le pouvoir non-démocratique communiste venait de détruire le mouvement indépendant Solidarność, qui, un an et demi auparavant, avait été établi, pour la première fois, dans une partie de l'Europe dominée par l'Union soviétique. Jean-Louis Baudouin m'a offert son appui dans un sens aussi bien métaphorique que très concret, en me prêtant de l'argent pour la première période de mon séjour à Montréal (à l'époque où les Polonais n'avaient droit qu'à 15 dollars en quittant leur pays), et il m'a surtout témoigné de son ouverture d'esprit, de son amitié et de son intérêt (certainement peu typique, surtout pour les élites intellectuelles) pour les évènements intervenus dans la partie de l'Europe dont je suis originaire. C'est précisément à ce moment que je me suis rendu compte de la personnalité exceptionnelle de Jean-Louis Baudouin : il donnait l'impression de tout savoir et de tout comprendre, en identifiant parfaitement et mieux que quiconque le drame vécu à l'époque par les sociétés oppressées sous le système communiste. C'était l'introduction à nos contacts très amicaux, qui se sont transformés ultérieurement en une coopération authentique sur le plan scientifique. Quand il m'a invité à assister à ses cours sur « Le progrès de la médecine et le droit », j'ai pu découvrir le style et la qualité inestimable de l'enseignement de Jean-Louis Baudouin. Ces cours ont représenté, par leurs formes, leurs contenus et les questions soulevées, une approche tout à fait nouvelle de l'analyse des problèmes juridiques. Ils ont fait la liaison entre, d'une part, la dimension éthico-philosophique et juridique et, d'autre part, l'analyse comparatiste, toutes deux reflétant les grandes découvertes de l'époque dans le domaine de la biologie et de la médecine. C'était à la fois de véritables spectacles d'érudition, reposant sur de profondes connaissances en la matière et plein d'humour, sans pour autant altérer la précision et la clarté des arguments présentés, tout en invitant à une passionnante discussion et à un débat ferme sur des questions fondamentales de droit et d'éthique. Car, il faut le dire, peu nombreux sont les Professeurs qui laissent un large espace à une discussion ouverte et égale avec les participants, en privilégiant un échange authentique avec leurs interlocuteurs, sans s'attribuer la position de mentor. Ces cours ont donc été pour moi une expérience émouvante et inédite.

Après quelques années, nous avons pu, avec l'aide du Centre de bioéthique de Montréal et avec la participation de son directeur, David Roy, réaliser un programme commun, inédit à l'époque, intitulé « Law and medicine. Canada and Poland in dialogue ». Cela a été une véritable expérience portée par deux visions différentes des grands problèmes de la médecine moderne et présentée par des philosophes, des juristes ainsi que des médecins. La conception de l'ouvrage issu de ce programme a été fondée sur la méthodologie typique de Jean-Louis Baudouin, à savoir une approche transversale et interdisciplinaire.

Dans les années 1980, j'ai bénéficié à plusieurs reprises de l'appui de Jean-Louis Baudouin, qui comprenait toujours parfaitement l'importance des contestations et des désobéissances sociales à l'égard du système totalitaire en place dans la partie Est de l'Europe et, lorsque le besoin s'en faisait sentir, il était toujours prêt à nous offrir son aide. Il était, pour ces raisons, un véritable « fan » de la transformation en cours dans mon pays et, à l'instar d'une grande partie de la société polonaise, il n'a jamais perdu l'espoir que l'unification de l'Europe sur la base des mêmes valeurs et principes devienne un jour possible.

Passons maintenant à certaines observations générales portant sur les écrits de Jean-Louis Baudouin. Il me semble pertinent, en tenant compte du contexte de cette cérémonie, de commencer par des réflexions qui concernent l'importance du droit comparé dans les travaux du Professeur Jean-Louis Baudouin. Il faut souligner surtout que celui-ci a parfaitement su profiter de la position exceptionnelle du droit privé au Québec, placé au croisement des deux grandes familles du droit contemporain, à savoir, d'une part, le droit civil, trouvant ses racines dans la culture juridique française, et, d'autre part, le système du common law. En effet, en dépit du fait que le Québec appartienne à la grande famille du droit civil, chaque juriste québécois est en même temps un juriste canadien qui, presque chaque jour, dans le cadre de sa pratique professionnelle, a l'occasion d'appliquer le droit fédéral et les systèmes juridiques en vigueur dans les autres provinces, fondés sur le common law. Autrement dit, les juristes québécois peuvent profiter de l'opportunité irremplaçable de pratiquer quotidiennement à la fois le droit privé et la common law et, par conséquent, de bien comprendre la nature des institutions juridiques qui appartiennent à chaque système, mais aussi d'identifier parfaitement les différences entre elles.

Parmi certains de nombreux ouvrages de Jean-Louis Baudouin, nous pouvons retrouver plusieurs observations de l'auteur sur les relations complexes entre le droit civil et le common law. Son jugement sur les conséquences de ce phénomène d'acculturation des différents systèmes juridiques dans le contexte québécois n'a pas été exclusivement positif. Dans les années 1960 (donc plusieurs années avant l'adoption du nouveau Code civil), il a écrit :

> Le système de droit privé québécois présente un intérêt incontestable pour une étude de sociologie juridique sur l'acculturation des pluralismes juridiques d'ordre externe. Notre droit privé est en effet presque totalement 'emprunté' au droit étranger. Cependant, le problème de l'assimilation des sources étrangères se complique singulièrement si l'on songe que, d'une part, on retrouve dans le Code civil des règles directement importées du droit anglais ou américain et que, d'autre part, le droit judiciaire privé québécois, tant au point de vue des règles de procédures que des techniques du jugement et de la nature du procès, provient en ligne droite du common law à quelques exceptions près. [...] La coexistence au sein du droit privé de deux pensées juridiques, de deux techniques, de deux influences aussi opposées, loin d'être un facteur de progrès, a été beaucoup plus un facteur d'abâtardissement du droit civil (Baudouin 1966, 403).

Cette situation québécoise constitue une invitation exceptionnelle aux recherches comparatistes mais, il faut le dire, peu de juristes savent et veulent profiter de cette invitation. Jean-Louis Baudouin, de son côté, est devenu l'un des plus éminents spécialistes de la méthode comparatiste dans le domaine de la recherche sur le droit civil et le common law. Ses analyses les plus intéressantes semblent être celles portant sur les différences entre l'application des mécanismes de ces grandes familles juridiques, l'interdépendance de ces dernières et leur influence mutuelle ainsi que, enfin, celles portant sur le rôle du juge dans ces deux systèmes. Citons donc l'auteur :

> Dans le système civiliste traditionnel, la légitimité est incarnée par le législateur et non par le juge. Ce dernier ne fait qu'appliquer, en principe, une norme démocratiquement décidée par les représentants du peuple démocratiquement élus. Que le magistrat soit d'accord ou non avec celle-ci importe peu. Certes, bien évidemment, dans la réalité des choses, il faut reconnaître que le juge peut, grâce à son pouvoir d'interprétation des textes, faire, défaire ou modifier substantiellement la volonté législative. Dans le système de common law traditionnel, la légitimité est, en l'absence de textes clairs et précis (et faut-il dire parfois même en leur présence) avant tout celle du juge. C'est lui, en effet, qui non seulement dit mais, dans bien des cas, créé la norme. Or, le magistrat n'est pas élu, ne représente pas l'État, encore moins le pouvoir politique. Il ne représente que lui-même. L'absence de législation l'oblige donc à décider de la normativité à la place du Parlement [. . .] Enfin, un effet pervers de ce 'gouvernement par les juges' est devant des sujets aussi délicats et controversés, pour le pouvoir ou le gouvernement, de s'abstenir de légiférer en raison des risques politiques qu'il court en prenant lui-même position et, partant, de déléguer une tâche normalement dévolue au Parlement au pouvoir judiciaire (Baudouin 2006, 96–97).

La réflexion de Jean-Louis Baudouin exprimée dans cette courte citation montre avec une grande clarté dans quelle mesure l'approche normative (typique du droit civil) ou l'approche judiciaire (typique de la common law) pourrait être préférable pour résoudre les grandes questions de nos sociétés contemporaines, parmi lesquelles celles en matière de bioéthique relèvent des plus délicates et des plus difficiles. En même temps, cette citation, qui soulève le dilemme du gouvernement des juges, constitue une petite leçon sur les conséquences découlant de différentes approches pour le fonctionnement de nos systèmes démocratiques et la légitimité de ceux-ci.

Dans une autre publication (Baudouin 1997, 283 et s.), Jean-Louis Baudouin exprime son pronostic selon lequel il est probable que la common law évoluera vers un système civiliste et un modèle de codification plutôt que l'inverse, certaines codifications dans le système de common law, telle que l'Uniform Commercial Code aux États-Unis, en étant l'exemple. Jean-Louis Baudouin souligne cet effort vers la codification, qui marque une rationalisation et une systématisation typique du système civiliste romaniste. Il ajoute qu'« il me semble qu'on cherchera de moins en moins la solution aux problèmes complexes dans la compilation et l'exégèse d'une multitude de décisions jurisprudentielles ».

Personnellement, je ne peux m'empêcher, depuis ma perspective actuelle de juge à la Cour de justice de l'Union européenne, confronté chaque jour à des problèmes délicats et complexes concernant la relation entre la langue et le droit, de noter à quel point l'observation de Jean-Louis Baudouin est pertinente quant aux relations entre la common law et le droit civil sur le plan linguistique. D'une part, Jean-Louis Baudouin aperçoit que si « le véhicule linguistique sert sans aucun doute de support, celui-ci est loin d'avoir, à notre époque, l'importance qu'on lui prête parfois. Le droit est bien plus que la langue, il a des racines beaucoup plus profondes dans la culture et la vie d'un peuple ». D'autre part, il souligne, à juste titre, la valeur ajoutée de la dualité linguistique et de la pratique de la common law en français (en l'occurrence au Nouveau Brunswick), qui se manifeste par l'impact visible sur la common law de la méthode civiliste qui est « autant sur le plan de la rédaction que de l'interprétation, [et qui est] un véhicule important de l'influence éventuelle des concepts et de la méthodologie civilistes en common law ». Mes expériences au Luxembourg me permettent de constater que le chevauchement des méthodologies civilistes et de la common law constitue, dans la pratique de la Cour de justice, notre « pain quotidien » et je ne peux que confirmer l'existence d'influences mutuelles remarquables parmi ces deux approches si nous prenons en compte, d'une part, l'importance de la jurisprudence, les avancées jurisprudentielles de la Cour, le souci permanent des juges d'assurer la cohérence et la continuité de la jurisprudence et, d'autre part, les travaux de plus en plus développés du législateur européen qui déterminent significativement notre effort d'interprétation et qui nous poussent à suivre la méthode civiliste. Je vois encore une autre coïncidence entre les observations remarquables de Jean-Louis Baudouin et mes expériences à la Cour, à savoir l'impact visible des grands principes découlant de la Charte des droits fondamentaux (au Canada et dans l'Union européenne) sur le processus entier d'interprétation et d'application du droit. Cette méthodologie fondée sur le postulat de rechercher toujours l'interprétation la plus proche et la plus conforme aux valeurs et à l'axiologie des droits fondamentaux devient une caractéristique de la pratique aussi bien dans le système du droit civil que dans celui de la common law. Par ailleurs, une telle méthodologie découle clairement de l'universalisme des droits fondamentaux. Par conséquent, elle constitue l'élément essentiel, l'héritage commun, permettant de rapprocher encore plus les deux grands systèmes de droit.

Les traits les plus marquants des écrits de Jean-Louis Baudouin, qui portent aussi bien sur le droit civil, le droit médical, la bioéthique ou la théorie générale et la méthodologie du droit, se manifestent par la clarté et la beauté interne de la structure et de la logique de l'argumentation, qui prouvent la virtuosité remarquable de l'auteur. La création doctrinale de Jean-Louis Baudouin peut servir d'exemple de «l'esthétique juridique», en comprenant tous les éléments pour construire un édifice à la fois simple et complexe, très bien équilibré et frappant par sa force d'expression.

Jean-Louis Baudouin joue de plusieurs instruments dans son « orchestre juridique », en explorant tous les possibilités pour trouver le mode d'expression le plus adéquat. Aussi bien la méthodologie utilisée par Jean-Louis Baudouin dans ses ouvrages que la matière juridique qu'il présente sont donc très différenciées et riches. Sa finesse de virtuose lui permet de choisir à chaque fois les meilleurs outils pour assurer un degré satisfaisant d'exploration. La méthodologie de Jean-Louis Baudouin constitue une palette diversifiée parmi laquelle nous trouvons des approches à la fois sociologiques, philosophiques, morales mais aussi dogmatiques et formelles, fondées sur la rigueur stricte de la logique juridique. La réponse cherchée par Jean-Louis Baudouin dans ses ouvrages n'est jamais limitée à une présentation simple du contenu des normes, n'est jamais « textuelle », mais prend toujours pour objectif principal de faire connaissance (savoir) avec tel ou tel mécanisme juridique dans sa complexité, y compris ses racines sociales, ses fonctions, son utilité, son effectivité, sa pratique jurisprudentielle, sa place dans les systèmes juridiques contemporains et, enfin, son évolution prochaine et les éventuelles corrections nécessaires.

Cette diversification et la richesse des œuvres de Jean-Louis Baudouin sont confirmées, comme il a déjà été constaté, par la pluralité des champs de ses recherches. Jean-Louis Baudouin, étant civiliste par son origine et par ses fascinations primordiales, est entré courageusement dans la pluralité des domaines et des branches du droit, en évitant une catégorisation facile de ses œuvres selon le critère de la spécialisation juridique.

Sans doute, l'étendue des explorations scientifiques entreprises par Jean-Louis Baudouin est puissante et exceptionnelle : dans la matière du droit privé surtout, des obligations et de la responsabilité délictuelle, dans le droit médical et la bioéthique, presque toutes les grandes questions sont discutées à partir des problèmes de procréation médicalement assistée par l'expérimentation sur l'être humain jusqu'à la problématique de la mort, de la cessation du traitement et de l'euthanasie. Sa passion scientifique, à côté des deux champs les plus importants de ses écrits (le droit privé et le droit médical et bioéthique), couvre également de nombreuses questions, très actuelles pour le débat public contemporain, présentées dans des articles dont les titres eux-mêmes parlent de la fascination scientifique de son auteur : La Société face au crime (1970), Terrorisme et justice (1970), Réflexions sur la codification comme mode d'expression de la règle de droit (1984), Démocratie, l'identité incertaine : la crise du droit (1993), Droits de la personne: Les bio-droits, Conclusions et Rapports de synthèse (1997).

Il ne reste qu'à ajouter que cette diversification et cette pluralité de recherches juridiques dans le monde contemporain constituent une rareté et même une exception. Une grande majorité des juristes, non seulement les praticiens mais aussi ceux qui viennent des milieux universitaires, font le choix d'une spécialisation de plus en plus étroite et stricte. Cependant, il n'y a aucun doute que, à l'époque actuelle, c'est l'exceptionnalité de l'approche choisie par Jean-Louis Baudouin qui désigne la route la plus correcte pour toutes les explorations juridiques. En effet, les frontières entre les domaines et les branches du droit deviennent de plus en plus floues, les interférences mutuelles des instruments juridiques appartenant à des disciplines diverses constituent une caractéristique commune aux solutions juridiques adoptées par les législateurs contemporains. Personne ne peut donc être étonné aujourd'hui par le phénomène clairement visible de « publicisation » du droit privé et de la «privatisation» du droit public, ou encore de la constitutionnalisation de ces deux grandes branches du droit sous le prisme des droits fondamentaux. A l'époque actuelle de globalisation et de confrontation permanente à de nouveaux défis, qui exigent une flexibilité et nécessitent d'introduire des instruments atypiques qui ne sont pas dans la continuation simple des voies déjà érigées et bien connues, l'approche pluraliste et interdisciplinaire, qui permet de dépasser le cloisonnement des branches du droit instauré par le développement linéaire du droit, semble être l'outil le plus adapté. Pour ces raisons, cela ne constitue pas une exagération de dire que l'enseignement de Jean-Louis Baudouin contient, par la diversification des matières et des méthodes d'analyse, un message particulièrement important adressé aux juristes contemporains appartenant aux différentes spécialisations ou même aux différentes familles juridiques.

À la question suivante : « Qui est d'abord Jean-Louis Baudouin? Un savant, un juriste un civiliste, un théoricien et philosophe, un comparatiste, un bio-éthicien et un spécialiste de droit médical ? », la réponse correcte est que Jean-Louis Baudouin est un spécialiste dans chacun de ces domaines, tout en se distinguant des spécialistes qui représentent ces domaines. Jean-Louis Baudouin reste toujours une personnalité n'ayant pas d'équivalent, dans son style et dans l'étendue des matières explorées, qui lui permettent d'orchestrer des approches et des instruments diversifiés, tous répondant à l'impératif de progresser dans la connaissance et dans la compréhension ainsi que d'expliquer de manière plus aboutie la complexité des sujets.

La bioéthique et le droit médical se sont trouvés depuis plusieurs années, comme souligné ci-dessus, au centre des fascinations scientifiques de Jean-Louis Baudouin. Les questions qu'il a posées dans ce contexte portent surtout sur la méthodologie qui doit être adoptée pour aborder, au sein du droit, la complexité des effets du développement scientifique. Le droit est-il susceptible de trouver une approche propre et autonome en répondant aux défis soulevés par les sciences ? À quel degré la science peut-elle déterminer des solutions et des mécanismes juridiques ? Est-il possible de maintenir la pluralité et la diversité des systèmes juridiques face à l'universalisme de la science? La méthodologie appliquée par le common law et le droit civil pour chercher les solutions adéquates est-elle similaire ? Quelle est la nature des relations entre la morale, l'éthique et le droit?

Jean-Louis Baudouin a développé des réflexions qui confrontent toutes ces questions dans un ouvrage écrit en coopération avec Catherine Labrusse–Riou, intitulé « Produire l'homme: de quel droit ? Étude juridique et éthique des procréations artificielles » (Paris 1987), qui a été à l'époque l'un des premiers essais entrés si profondément dans la matière, sans éviter les problèmes les plus sensibles et complexes qui se posent.

L'une des valeurs ajoutées de cet ouvrage passionnant, qui retient notre attention, se trouve au sein des réflexions menées sur les relations entre les sciences, le droit, la morale et l'éthique.

Jean-Louis Baudouin a décrit très clairement sa position en utilisant des arguments convaincants: le droit a son propre rôle à jouer face aux conséquences des développements scientifiques. L'autonomie du droit doit être respectée si nous voulons maintenir sa signification et sa portée comme faisant partie de notre culture et de nos traditions fondées sur un long processus de développement. Les questions qui se posent aux juristes sont cependant extrêmement complexes : « La tâche des juristes est donc lourde et comme chaque fois qu'ils se trouvent confrontés à des questions neuves et conflictuelles, ils sont contraints de faire preuve à la fois de réalisme et d'idéalisme, de n'être ni anges, ni bêtes, ni courtisans de la science, ni voix de la théologie » (p. 252). Plus loin, les auteurs ajoutent une réflexion très juste en annonçant le risque d'une confusion des rôles et, par conséquent, d'une déformation de la vocation d'une part, de la science et, d'autre part, du droit : « Les juristes sont aujourd'hui, plus qu'autrefois, dans une situation intenable. A l'inverse de la science, instance de vérité relative, le droit est instance de jugement. Or, l'empire des sciences conduit celles-ci, malgré elles, à s'instituer comme l'instance de légitimité qu'elles ne sont pas, tandis que le droit, dépouillé de ses capacités de jugement, tend à être l'instance de vérité, qu'il n'est pas » (p. 278-279).

Ces avertissements donnés par les auteurs il y a trente ans sont toujours actuels et même encore plus actuels aujourd'hui quand « la production de l'homme » se réalise à l'aide de moyens et d'instruments beaucoup plus puissants et plus développés. Le droit a-t-il déjà trouvé ou découvert son propre rôle pour assurer la cohérence et la continuité de nos grandes traditions enracinées dans notre culture juridique fondée sur le respect de la dignité humaine et le respect de chaque individu dans son intégrité ? Sommes-nous suffisamment préparés pour répondre aux défis actuels soulevés par le progrès scientifique permanent et de plus en plus dynamique ? Sans doute, la réponse est négative et, pour cette raison, nous avons besoin de revenir plus que jamais à ces questions fondamentales, qui restent très actuelles, pour ne pas dire urgentes. Cette approche serait-elle la seule voie pour suivre le message exprimé par Jean-Louis Baudouin et Catherine Labrusse–Riou lorsqu'ils ont rappelé notre responsabilité prochaine, afin de « rendre la vie vivable non seulement pour le présent mais pour l'avenir et les générations futures qui seront en droit de nous demander des comptes de notre démesure » (p. 280) ?

Les questions qui se posent en matière de bioéthique restent aussi particulièrement intéressantes du point de vue du droit comparé et surtout si nous voulons aborder le problème de l'adéquation des méthodes proposées par le système de common law, d'une part, et les systèmes de droit civil, d'autre part, pour se saisir des grands défis évoqués par le progrès scientifique. Doit-on privilégier la méthode de l'intervention législative, par laquelle est recherché l'équilibre et la cohérence générale du système, ou bien des développements par le biais de la jurisprudence, donc par des systèmes qui placent les juges au centre de grands débats publics en les autorisant à adapter leurs réponses au cas par cas en fonction des circonstances individuelles de chaque espèce ? Les réflexions de Jean-Louis Baudouin et de Catherine Labrusse–Riou montrent clairement qu'il n'y a pas une seule méthodologie « du droit à créer » parce qu'elle « peut dépendre de la structure propre de chaque système juridique, ou du rôle imparti à la déontologie médicale dans chaque État » (p. 269). Dans les deux systèmes, les difficultés sont présentes: « les systèmes de droit écrit et codifié sont liés avec la crise des codifications due à l'inflation débordante des lois, décrets, règlements ou circulaires [. . ..], qui risquent d'être obsolètes au lendemain de leur publication » (p. 270) et les systèmes du common law où « les grands débats sur la bioéthique trouvent devant les juridictions et spécialement dans la jurisprudence constitutionnelle l'occasion de s'exprimer et de se développer [. . .] la cohérence des solutions n'y trouve pas toujours son compte » (p. 271).

L'une des caractéristiques des écrits de Jean-Louis Baudouin dans le domaine de la théorie du droit civil mérite d'être spécialement mise en évidence, à savoir ses réflexions sur la relation entre le milieu social et l'évolution du droit. Cette question, qui reste très actuelle et importante pour l'élaboration de la stratégie d'adaptation du droit aux besoins actuels, s'éloigne de plus en plus des instruments traditionnels créés au cours de la période d'évolution stable et lente des systèmes juridiques. Actuellement, ces changements sont dynamiques et les défis sont énormes pour les législateurs contemporains: le processus d'adaptation du droit doit-il être immédiat pour répondre au plus vite aux attentes des différents milieux sociaux ou bien doit-il suivre une stratégie raisonnable qui se manifeste par des changements graduels, précédés par l'identification claire des phénomènes sociaux exigeant une réaction du législateur ? Faut-il distinguer de ce point de vue entre le droit civil et le droit public ? Écoutons l'auteur qui nous présente une réflexion intéressante en la matière :

> Il est nécessaire auparavant de préciser qu'au point de vue sociologique, il est évident que le droit civil, peut-être plus que le droit public, est nécessairement en retard par rapport à la réalité sociale. Ce déphasage est inévitable puisque le juridique étant un produit du social ne peut se cristalliser dans une norme définie qu'en autant que le besoin social s'en fait ressentir d'une manière suffisamment forte. La règle de droit civil ne peut pratiquement jamais être imposée. Il lui faut avant tout être acceptée et ressentie par le milieu social auquel elle s'adresse. Le législateur en droit privé peut rarement se permettre de faire des lois qui veulent innover pour l'avenir mais doit se contenter de coucher dans une sorte de lit de Procuste de la réalité sociale la règle de droit privé. Encore faut-il qu'il n'accumule pas trop de retard et ne laisse pas le fossé s'agrandir entre le droit civil et la réalité sociologique (Baudouin 1966, 393). [...] La transmutation en règle juridique d'un besoin social de réforme est forcément lente car le droit civil n'est là que pour l'ensemble de la population. La règle doit donc représenter autant que possible la normalité de la conscience sociale (passim, 394).

La grande valeur des écrits de Jean-Louis Baudouin dans le domaine du droit civil, surtout pour ce qui concerne le droit des obligations et la responsabilité délictuelle, donc portant sur l'essence du droit privé, reflète sans doute son art de la synthèse et sa clarté exemplaire, rarement rencontrés parmi les juristes qui, en principe, préfèrent se cacher derrière un mur de complexités et de raisonnements extrêmement développés et peu compréhensibles. Pour Jean-Louis Baudouin, la manière de présenter une matière et l'esprit de synthèse sont une exigence encore plus importante à l'époque actuelle, qui favorise systématiquement la complexité et le nombre des règles normatives produites par les législateurs. La manière adoptée par Jean-Louis Baudouin pour expliquer les institutions de droit privé est certainement l'une des raisons pour lesquelles ses manuels académiques profitent d'une telle popularité et d'un tel succès parmi les étudiants. Dans ce contexte, on ne peut pas être étonné de l'observation de Jean-Louis Baudouin adressée aux jeunes juristes qui se préparent à exercer la profession d'avocat :

> La capacité de synthèse, aussi, est importante, d'autant plus que beaucoup de procès sont très compliqués. Il faut arriver à simplifier les choses de façon correcte (L'interview: Le défi d'être juge selon Jean-Louis Baudouin, DROIT-INC du 23 Juin 2010).

Sont impressionnants ce degré de clarté, la pertinence, la précision avec lesquelles Jean-Louis Baudouin a identifié et a toujours présenté les grandes tendances et les grandes évolutions du droit civil. Prenons quelques exemples à partir de son ouvrage portant sur la responsabilité délictuelle, écrit il y a trente ans, où sont identifiées très précisément toutes les grandes caractéristiques des approches modernes du droit privé en la matière et qui restent, en dépit de l'écoulement du temps, toujours actuelles et clairement confirmées par l'évolution de nos systèmes juridiques dans les dernières années. Ces observations concernaient la prolifération de régimes particuliers de responsabilité fondés sur la garantie, le risque ou la sécurité sociale générale. On ne peut que partager l'opinion très pertinente de Jean-Louis Baudouin, qui identifie aussi dans ce contexte l'évolution parallèle de la notion de faute civile marquée par les standards afin de déterminer une conduite civilement fautive. « Cet abaissement des standards est probablement dû à un changement d'attitude de leur part [les tribunaux] qui reflète une différence de perception générale du rôle de la responsabilité. Les tribunaux tolèrent de moins en moins, surtout en matière de dommages corporels, qu'une personne blessée reste sans compensation. Ils se satisfont donc plus facilement qu'il y a un siècle de l'existence d'une faute leur permettant d'octroyer une indemnité ». L'auteur ajoute une remarque plus générale concernant le développement d'une tendance vers l'objectivisation de la responsabilité :

> En supprimant le débat sur la faute, en ôtant le recours aux tribunaux judicaires et en 'administrativisant' le recours, la compensation (même si elle reste inférieure à celle à laquelle la victime aura en vertu du droit commun), peut être accordée plus rapidement (Baudouin 1973, 26).

Bon exemple de style « baudouinien », nous y trouvons aussi une observation synthétique qui porte sur les controverses et le débat doctrinal concernant l'unité des deux responsabilités civiles (contractuelle et délictuelle). En identifiant un phénomène moderne de responsabilité civile marqué par le fait que les frontières parmi ces deux concepts (contractuel et délictuel) s'estompent de plus en plus, il explique en deux phrases la différence qui demeure entre eux, en dépit de toutes les similarités existantes :

> Une seule différence sépare les deux. Alors qu'en règle générale, la responsabilité délictuelle résulte du manquement à une obligation de ne pas faire, permanente et légale, la responsabilité contractuelle peut résulter d'une contravention à une obligation de faire, de donner, ou de ne pas faire, est temporaire et prend sa source dans un acte juridique (Baudouin 1973, 12).

Pour Jean-Louis Baudouin, être juriste signifie nécessairement faire respecter la justice d'une façon qui permette l'utilisation d'instruments d'interprétation du droit suffisamment flexibles, adaptés aux circonstances sociales actuelles, fondées sur les grands principes du droit trouvés dans le système de droit tout entier, dans une perspective large, et non très formelle et étroite, mais aussi du point de vue de la lecture textuelle. L'un des principaux objectifs qui doit guider l'activité des juristes, et notamment les magistrats, est, dans le domaine du droit privé, d'essayer de construire une nouvelle moralité contractuelle, fondée sur des éléments d'équité et d'équilibre, donc sur des valeurs qui trouvent leurs racines dans la notion d'« aequitas » du droit romain. Pour Jean-Louis Baudouin,

> Le pouvoir judiciaire détient [donc] maintenant tous les outils nécessaires pour le contrôle de cette nouvelle moralité contractuelle. La capacité d'intervention des tribunaux dans les diverses étapes de la vie du contrat fait désormais de ceux-ci les véritables maîtres de l'équité contractuelle. L'idéal de justice, l'humanisation des rapports conventionnels restent un objectif à long terme qu'il leur appartiendra de développer au cours des années à venir. À cet égard, il faut souhaiter que, délaissant le conservatisme des années 60 et 70 précédemment souligné, les magistrats fassent preuve, au contraire, d'une ouverture d'esprit et donnent aux nouveaux textes une interprétation large et contextuelle. Il faut également souhaiter une meilleure structuration de la réflexion judiciaire. Pour ne pas tout confondre et tout banaliser, un effort de réflexion doit être entrepris pour tracer les frontières respectives de la bonne foi, de l'équité et de l'abus de droit [...] (Baudouin 2015, 44).

Dans cette petite citation, Jean-Louis Baudouin nous a transmis son message concernant le rôle des juges qui, pour lui, en tant que Professeur de droit, ayant également une expérience au sein de plus haute juridiction du Québec, reste l'essence de l'activité de juriste. Dans une interview donnée il y a quelques années, Jean-Louis Baudouin, à la question posée par le journaliste : « Quel est le plus grand défi professionnel auquel vous avez fait face ? », répond sans hésitation : « Je dirais que le plus grand défi était d'être juge. Le premier défi est de développer une connaissance générale de l'ensemble des sphères du droit, alors qu'on est spécialisé dans certains domaines. Ce qui implique donc une mise à jour des connaissances sur le plan juridique, mais aussi du point de vue éthique et moral » (L'interview : Le défi d'être juge selon Jean-Louis Baudouin, DROIT-INC du 23 Juin 2010). Nous pouvons ajouter que, parmi les Professeurs de droit, il n'y a pas beaucoup de représentants de la profession qui sont « plus » aptes que lui à exercer la fonction de juge, par sa sensibilité et sa parfaite compréhension du sens de cette activité et, parmi les juges, il n'y en a pas beaucoup qui sont « plus » préparés que lui pour passer d'un domaine du droit à un autre grâce à une large vision du système de droit.

Par cette observation, nous voudrions terminer l'éloge du Professeur Jean-Louis Baudouin. Dans cette courte intervention, seuls quelques éléments de la richesse des écrits et de l'activité de Jean-Louis Baudouin ont été présentés ! Pour finir, il ne me reste qu'à te prier, cher Jean-Louis Baudouin, de ma part et au nom de l'Académie Internationale de droit comparé, d'accepter mes sincères félicitations et mes meilleurs souhaits dans la poursuite de ton activité fascinante, le plus longtemps possible.

Références

Baudouin JL (1966) Le Code civil québécois: crise de croissance ou crise de vieillesse. Can Bar Rev 44:391–416

Baudouin JL (1973) La Responsabilité civile délictuelle, les presses de l'Université de Montréal

Baudouin JL (1997) Quelques réflexions d'un civiliste sur la common law pluriel. Revue de la common law en français 1997:283–290

Baudouin JL (2006) Common law, droit civil: réflexions sur les outils du juge en bioéthique. Journal International de Bioéthique 17:95–102

Baudouin JL (2015) Justice et équilibre: La nouvelle moralité contractuelle du droit civil québécois, dans: Études offertes à Jacques Ghestin. Le contrat au début de XXIème siècle, Paris, 2015, p 44

Remerciements/Acknowledgments

Jean-Louis Baudouin

Laissez-moi tout d'abord remercier Madame la Présidente et Monsieur le Secrétaire général de l'Académie pour cet honneur auquel je suis particulièrement sensible.

Merci aussi à mon cher ami Marek Safjan. Je mets les éloges dont il m'a comblé sur le compte de la grande et fidèle amitié qui existe entre nous depuis il y a déjà plusieurs décennies. Marek était venu à Montréal, à la Faculté de droit pour un séjour de quelques mois en 1982 alors que j'y étais professeur. C'était une période très difficile pour lui alors qu'il débutait sa carrière professorale. La Pologne, en effet, commençait à espérer pouvoir se sortir de la dictature communiste grâce au mouvement Solidarność. D'ailleurs, Marek n'avait reçu l'autorisation de quitter son pays qu'à condition d'y laisser femme et enfants.

Par la suite, j'ai eu la chance d'aller donner des cours à la Faculté de droit de Varsovie grâce à lui, puis, avec d'autres, d'y créer une antenne nouvelle de bioéthique. J'ai pu alors faire la connaissance de collègues polonais exceptionnels comme Andrej Muzjinowski et être témoin un petit peu de cette période critique de l'histoire de la Pologne. Grâce à Marek, j'ai pu en effet assister à ce moment très fort et très émouvant qu'a été la célébration de la messe par le pape Jean-Paul II (le « polonais ») dans le grand stade de Varsovie.

Après la chute de la dictature communiste, Marek a connu une brillante carrière d'abord à l'Université, puis comme juge et président du Tribunal constitutionnel polonais. Il est maintenant, comme vous le savez tous, juge à la Cour de justice de Luxembourg. Il a réussi à combiner d'une part une remarquable vivacité intellectuelle et d'autre part, un sens aigu de ses responsabilités sociales dans l'exercice de la judicature.

Merci Marek, merci de tes bons mots à mon égard. Merci surtout de la fidèle amitié.

J.-L. Baudouin (✉)
Faculté de droit de l'Université de Montréal, Avocat-conseil Fasken, Montréal, QC, Canada
e-mail: jbaudouin@fasken.com

K. Boele-Woelki, D. P. Fernàndez Arroyo (eds.), *The Past, Present and Future of Comparative Law - Le passé, le présent et le futur du droit comparé*, Ius Comparatum – Global Studies in Comparative Law 29, https://doi.org/10.1007/978-3-319-93770-0_12

Partie V / Part V
Rodolfo Sacco

Le passé, le présent et le futur du droit comparé

Rodolfo Sacco

Je crois que pendant plus de mille ans le juriste s'était interdit de comparer. De tout temps, la vision des systèmes de droit différents l'un de l'autre aurait pu susciter la comparaison, mais depuis deux mille ans la comparaison ne pouvait pas être l'affaire du juriste.

Si le juriste est convaincu qu'un seul modèle juridique est bien conçu et partant légitime, ce juriste sait que son propre système est légitime, il en déduit que tous les autres systèmes se composent de fausses règles. Ces fausses règles (indûment considérées comme juridiques dans tel ou tel malheureux pays), ces fausses règles rebelles à Dieu, ou rebelles à la raison, ou à la nature – ont enfreint l'ordre qui doit être à la base du droit.

Il y a presque mille ans, l'on a commencé à voir dans les universités les lieux où l'on connaissait – et par conséquent le lieu où l'on apprenait – le droit, et le droit qu'on y enseignait était le corpus juris de Justinien, à qui Dieu avait confié la tâche de mettre par écrit le droit. Pouvons-nous faire de comparaison entre un savoir divin et la volonté d'un prince ou des créations du peuple ? Le professeur savait qu'un droit coutumier existait partout, mais, s'il en parlait, il le baptisait « Ius Asininum » qui personne n'aurait jamais comparé un droit, que Dieu nous a donné, à la charî'a islamique, produite par l'imagination d'un abominable faux-prophète. Et pour une raison réciproque, le faqîh islamique s'intéressait peu au droit des «muissa».

Au fil des siècles la société s'est sécularisée, et la vision du droit en a été bouleversée. Le savant s'inspire désormais des lumières, il est à la recherche de la solution juridique dictée par la raison.

R. Sacco (✉)
Università di Torino, Torino, Italy
e-mail: domenico.dimicco@unito.it

K. Boele-Woelki, D. P. Fernàndez Arroyo (eds.), *The Past, Present and Future of Comparative Law - Le passé, le présent et le futur du droit comparé*, Ius Comparatum – Global Studies in Comparative Law 29, https://doi.org/10.1007/978-3-319-93770-0_13

Je ne réussis pas à imaginer un juriste qui aurait conçu et entrepris une analyse comparative d'un droit rationnel et du droit des Pandectes. La comparaison présuppose l'idée d'une pluralité de droits tous également légitimes, et cette idée, inattendue, jusqu'au moment donné se lève à partir du jour dans lequel le romantisme a vu le droit comme le produit des diverses cultures, produit qui est – à juste titre – variable et multiple, car les cultures sont variées et multiples. Le personnage sur le devant de la scène est ici von Savigny.

Il faudra du temps, pour que la comparaison se développe. Il faudra du temps pour qu'on comprenne quelle est la richesse du savoir que la comparaison peut offrir, quelles sont les méthodes à suivre, quelles sont les conditions à remplir pour que la comparaison donne ses fruits.

Les premières manifestations d'un intérêt pour le droit des autres se trouvent dans le secteur de l'ethnologie juridique, notamment avec Morgan, Maine, Post. Je parle du dix-neuvième siècle. En cette époque la diversité acquiert droit de cité même dans le domaine de la linguistique, qui commence à adopter une vision comparative de toutes les langues.

Mais revenons au droit. Avec le commencement du XX siècle, à la légitimité du droit de l'autre sont offerts des témoignages bien savants. En France, Saleilles et Lambert apprennent à leurs compatriotes les secrets du droit allemand et du droit anglais.

Vers la moitié du siècle, commencent à être en formation des écoles postuniversitaires, nées pour enseigner le droit comparé. J'aime à rappeler, ici, la Faculté internationale pour l'enseignement du droit comparé, qui œuvrait à Strasbourg. J'aime à rappeler ici un personnage: Felipe de Solá Cañizares.

Dans cette même époque, la science est en marche. René David met un peu d'ordre dans ce thème à l'étendue infinie, et pour faire cela il construit le schéma des diverses familles de systèmes juridique. Schlesinger et Gorla étudient le contrat en droit comparé, et – pour opérer une comparaison valable – ils contrôlent (pour chaque système considéré) quelle est la correspondance entre les textes de loi, les applications qu'en fait la jurisprudence et l'interprétation qui est enseignée dans les écoles. La comparaison a ainsi généré une révision de la théorie des sources du droit. En même temps, son œil bien ouvert sur l'application du droit a comporté l'abandon de la conception statique du droit. Pour le juriste qui identifie le droit à la loi, le droit « est » un tel. La comparaison nous demande de considérer que le droit n'« est » pas, il « devient » !

Il y a plus. La comparaison – c'est évident – a approfondi le thème de la circulation des modèles. Et c'est elle, qui a proposé le thème de la latence dans le droit, c'est-à-dire, le thème des règles qui sont actives dans la vie du droit, sans que personne n'en perçoive l'existence.

Et la comparaison est en train de nous adresser des promesses. Nous ne pouvons pas connaître tout le futur de notre science. Mais nous voyons bien qu'elle commence à affronter des thèmes d'un intérêt extrême.

Le comparatiste traduit. Il traduit sans cesse, et il traduit des mots qui parlent du droit. Mais le linguiste nous confirme que le mot juridique – le signifiant - n'a pas un correspondant dans la réalité qui précède, chronologiquement, le mot.

Dans les sciences naturelles, je parle d'éléphant à quelqu'un qui a toujours vu l'éléphant. Dans le droit, si je parle du tribunal, je parle de quelque chose qui a existé à partir du moment dans lequel a été conçue l'idée du tribunal, et pas avant. Cela signifie que dans une langue je ne trouve pas, en principe, le mot pour traduire le terme juridique d'une autre langue. Que faire ? Les comparatistes sont en train de prendre en charge ces problèmes. Ils ont créé les bases d'un nouveau savoir: la traductologie juridique.

L'anthropologie culturelle s'occupe de thèmes – tels que la famille et le conflit – qui intéressent le juriste. Et voilà que les comparatistes se penchent sur ces thèmes, et naît l'anthropologie du droit. Vanderlinden, Rouland, Macdonald sont les premiers exemples de ce que je dis.

Il faut encore ajouter que les comparatistes ont compris l'importance qu'ont, pour eux, certains secteurs du savoir. Et nous pouvons imaginer que bientôt quelqu'un d'entre eux s'adonnera à toutes les applications de ces savoirs qui peuvent être d'utilité pour le juriste.

Je pense à l'éthologie. Elle étudie le comportement social de l'homme et des animaux.

Je pense au cognitivisme, qui étudie les modes de connaissance pratiqués par les humains. L'homme peut se soumettre à une règle sans avoir pleine conscience de cette règle: des neurones lui suggèrent 'comment il doit faire' sans lui expliquer la formulation de la règle. En effet, quand nous voulons ouvrir la porte, nous la poussons avec la force nécessaire et pourtant nous ne saurions pas dire la mesure de la force nécessaire. On entrevoit que ces phénomènes ne sont pas sans intérêt pour le juriste.

J'estime que le comparatiste ne peut pas penser à un prochain futur oisif et reposant. Mais heureusement personne d'entre les nombreux comparatistes que je connais, ne rêve d'un prochain futur reposant et oisif.

Merci.

Rodolfo Sacco : l'intellectuel, le juriste, le comparatiste

Antonio Gambaro

Ce qui caractérise les grands comparatistes que nous honorons est que chacun d'eux a voulu être ce qu'il a été, et l'intentionnalité de l'action a été couronnée par le succès qu'aujourd'hui, mais non seulement aujourd'hui, nous reconnaissons.

En parlant de Rodolfo Sacco la première mise au point qui apparaît approprié est qu'il a voulu être un juriste et un intellectuel et il s'est éduqué aux tels rôles avec une ténacité constante, en interrompant la propre « Bildung » temporairement seulement pour mener l'activité de combattant partisan; activité, d'autre part, effectuée avec passion, intelligence et succès.

Il est opportun de rappeler aussi que la vocation pour le rôle de l'intellectuel fut précédente à celle pour le rôle de juriste, parce que quand il était jeune il était attiré par le métier de l'historien et puis il fut tenté par l'économie vers laquelle l'encourageait Luigi Einaudi.

Choisi cependant le métier de juriste, Rodolfo Sacco n'eut pas d'hésitations à se consacrer au droit civil en tant que discipline traditionnellement destinée à offrir à toutes les autres disciplines juridiques l'équipement intellectuel nécessaire à un travail scientifique.

Il faut aussi ajouter que Sacco a toujours conçu le rôle de juriste civiliste avec l'esprit critique propre de l'intellectuel. Comme ça, se mesurant initialement avec le sujet vertigineux de l'interprétation de la loi, il a souligné le rôle que dans le processus herméneutique est joué par l'esprit de l'interprète. Que cet élément soit essentiel est devenu aujourd'hui affirmation banale, mais à l'époque (1947) la subjectivité de l'interprète était considérée comme une hérésie.

A. Gambaro (✉)
University of Milano, Law Faculty, Milan, Italy
e-mail: antonio.gambaro@unimi.it

K. Boele-Woelki, D. P. Fernàndez Arroyo (eds.), *The Past, Present and Future of Comparative Law - Le passé, le présent et le futur du droit comparé*, Ius Comparatum – Global Studies in Comparative Law 29, https://doi.org/10.1007/978-3-319-93770-0_14

A vrai dire Sacco n'a jamais cherché l'hérésie pour le goût de la provocation. Au contraire il a mis en discussion seulement les narrations, ou les présentations théoriques incohérentes avec les données observables. Et il est essentiellement dans le mode de retrouver les données observables et dans la détermination des critères à travers lesquelles les transposer en narrations cohérentes que Rodolfo Sacco a exprimé sa propre créativité scientifique. Et ce fut aussi la recherche de données observables d'une manière scientifique qui l'a conduit au droit comparé, où la science du juriste peut se déployer dans la manière la plus adéquate.

L'œuvre de Sacco est très vaste; elle se compose de plus de vingt livres, la majeure partie desquels est traduite dans d'autres langues, ce qui fait de lui le juriste italien le plus traduit. Une bibliographie complète demanderait tellement de pages que ne peut pas être proposée ici. Donc, plus qu'aux données quantitatives il convient de faire référence aux aspects qualitatifs, en tenant compte des frontières multiples dans lesquelles la créativité scientifique de Rodolfo Sacco s'est révélée, à partir de sa formulation de la notion de formant du droit.

Dans une vision réaliste il faut admettre que chaque système juridique présente des contradictions à son propre intérieur. La réaction normale consiste à en souhaiter le dépassement. Sacco a mis en lumière comme des séquences de règles qui apparaissent contradictoires entre eux, puissent être ordonnées selon leur origine, en distinguant la séquence d'origine législative de celle d'origine doctorale et de celle d'origine jurisprudentielle. En effet législateurs, juges et professeurs sont des sujets agents qui peuvent poursuivre des objectifs différents qui se complètent entre eux dialectiquement. Dans cette dimension, la théorie des formants ne se préoccupe pas d'harmoniser les dicta des différents acteurs du *legal process* et accepte totalement la possibilité de contrastes, non seulement parce que c'est la description qui mieux s'adapte aux données observables, mais parce qu'elle reconnaît la valeur des divergences entre formants en tant facteur de la dynamique du système.

Le deuxième exemple de créativité scientifique que j'aimerais bien vous signaler concerne la notion de cryptotype.

Une des dimensions de la complexité juridique est due à la présence à l'intérieur de chaque expérience juridique de séquences de propositions normatives verbalisées de manière suffisamment claire, unies à propositions verbalisées de manière ambiguë, unies à segments de sens non verbalisés. Seulement à travers l'effet de contraste, permis par la comparaison juridique, il est possible de déchiffrer l'entrelacement entre ce qui est dit avec clarté suffisante, ce qui est dit de manière ambiguë et ce qui n'est pas du tout dit. Dans cet œuvre de déchiffrement du latent Sacco a été le Maestro. Ses études sur le consentement translatif et sur la remise abstraite sont devenues des classiques du droit savant européen.

La même approche scientifique vers l'étude de la phénoménologie de la latence a donné des fruits dans la reconstruction des phénomènes juridiques de longue durée. Dans ce contexte, on doit supposer que les règles de droit peuvent être dépassées, mais pas oublié définitivement et donc qu'elles se disposent en substrats qui concourent à former le contexte épistémologique dans lequel se placent les règles juridiques actuelles. L'enquête stratigraphique des systèmes du passé permet de mettre en lumière la persistance de fragments des substrats précédentes et aussi leur influence sur le présent, en permettant d'expliquer la longue durée de certains modes de penser pas complètement verbalisés.

L'approche stratigraphique s'est montrée fructueuse dans l'étude des traditions juridiques de l'Afrique sub-Saharienne et dans les études d'anthropologie juridique, mais il y a d'autres secteurs d'enquête scientifique auxquels Sacco a donné des contributions très significatives.

A ce propos j'aimerais bien vous offrir un troisième exemple.

Il y a à peine quelques décennies, même les comparatistes négligeaient les problèmes de traduction d'un langage juridique à un autre. Sacco dans l'Introduction au droit comparé de 1980 et puis dans l'édition française amplifiée de 1991 signale le sujet et il en fait l'objet de ses études. Par la suite il rend la traductologie juridique un domaine de recherche pour les juristes, domaine qui est aujourd'hui en pleine floraison. En effets les problèmes de traduction/transposition d'un langage juridique à un autre ont toujours existés, et ils ont toujours été des problèmes graves, importants et complexes, mais ils n'étaient pas aperçus en tant que tels et on ne disposait pas des instruments théoriques pour les analyser.

Le problème ne réside pas dans les fautes de traduction, qui sont des erreurs qui peuvent se produire. Ce qui est scientifiquement intéressant est plutôt la question de la perte, ou de l'agrandissement, de sens qui se vérifie quand un signe linguistique est transposé d'une langue de départ à une langue d'arrivée où on ne trouve pas une catégorie juridique parfaitement correspondante. Le contrat n'est pas le «contract» parce que l'ensemble des phénomènes juridiques qui sont classés dans les deux catégories diverge, et donc quand on traduit un signe avec l'autre se perdent ou s'ajoutent des sens qu'il faut identifier et dont il faut être bien conscient.

Plutôt, il faut rappeler les autres fronts sur lequel Sacco a opéré et il opère encore avec une énergie infatigable. La modernisation des études juridiques dans les facultés de droit; le soin dans le recrutement des jeunes spécialistes qu'il suit avec dévouement et art; le renouvellement de la littérature.

Je dois ajouter qu'aux frontières des études juridiques il n'a pas cessé d'être toujours attentif aux questions épistémologiques, parce que si le juriste peut être un systématiseur, l'intellectuel ne peut pas être autre qu'un explorateur et donc Sacco a toujours poursuivi l'objectif de perfectionner les instruments de connaissance du droit.

Et le voilà donc explorer dans les directions où nos connaissances étaient plus déficitaires : du droit des pays socialistes aux droits Africains; mais son vrai champ est l'épistémologie juridique en général, où il met au travail les compétences qu'il a acquis en lisant passionnément de linguistique, d'anthropologie, d'histoire et de préhistoire. Aux frontières de la connaissance juridique il découvre l'importance des actes pré-linguistiques, de l'exercice du pouvoir du fait comme acte d'autonomie, et il souligne qu'aussi le droit muet est un droit.

Et alors nous devons dire que Rodolfo Sacco est essentiellement un modèle d'intellectuel et de juriste pour tous ceux qui s'acheminent sur la rue de la connaissance scientifique des phénomènes institutionnels; route qui a une particularité : elle ne finit jamais.

Remerciements/Acknowledgements

Rodolfo Sacco

Quel prix d'honneur ! Quelle chance ! Quelle chance – après tout – imprévisible ! Inattendue !

Nous recevons le prix, et cela nous fait penser à tout le temps que nous avons consacré au droit comparé; dans mon cas, tout au long d'une activité de recherche et d'enseignement ininterrompue pendant soixante-dix ans.

Au commencement, les collègues des facultés italiennes ne comprenaient pas notre intérêt par la comparaison. Longtemps ils ont été contraires à l'introduction de cette perspective dans les plans d'études des facultés ou, du moins, ils voulaient réduire l'importance de cette perspective à un minimum.

Ils étaient fidèles au dogme qui identifiait le droit à la loi, ils voyaient l'État comme le créateur de la loi et donc du droit, sans le dire ils sous-entendaient que la fidélité à son propre État était compromise s'ils évoquaient – dans leurs cours – le droit étranger, donc la loi étrangère, donc l'État étranger et rival. Le doit étranger était un non-droit.

Quarante ans de travail pour convaincre, une après l'autre, sans cesse, les soixante-dix facultés de droit et, ensuite, les organes du ministère. Entre-temps, l'incompréhension, l'hostilité, l'ironie. L'on pensait que j'inventais un chapitre à moi du savoir juridique pour y avoir le monopole du pouvoir dans mon intérêt personnel et de mes disciples, de mon école, et tout cela au dépend de l'université.

Un jour un ministre a signé l'ordonnance. Depuis, la comparaison juridique est matière fondamentale et donne son nom à une branche importante du savoir juridique (pour la bureaucratie italienne, la branche 02).

R. Sacco (✉)
Università di Torino, Torino, Italy
e-mail: domenico.dimicco@unito.it

K. Boele-Woelki, D. P. Fernàndez Arroyo (eds.), *The Past, Present and Future of Comparative Law - Le passé, le présent et le futur du droit comparé*, Ius Comparatum – Global Studies in Comparative Law 29, https://doi.org/10.1007/978-3-319-93770-0_15

Et les facultés ont compris. Un jour j'ai fait des comptes, et j'ai vu que la faculté de Turin offrait à ses étudiants dix-neuf cours de droit comparé, la faculté de Florence en offrait dix-sept et la faculté de Trente, quinze.

Hier, l'ironie. Aujourd'hui, la cérémonie.

Je m'aperçois, à présent, que l'hostilité, les accusations, le mépris, avaient laissé une cicatrice qui me faisait souffrir. Mais voilà. Cette séance, qu'a voulue l'Académie de droit comparé, a guéri ma cicatrice, et j'en suis heureux.

La longue bataille avait laissé dans mon esprit une impression de poids et de fatigue. Et la présence des Amis et des Collègues qui siègent dans cette salle, ayant parcouru un peu moins, ou beaucoup plus, de mille kilomètres ont eu comme effet d'effacer cette impression et ce souvenir. Je suis heureux.

À mon âge, quatre-vingt-quatorze ans, je vois s'approcher le moment de me retirer des affaires, et dresser un bilan des chances et malchances de mon aventure.

Et à la cérémonie voulue par l'Académie, et à la distinction qui m'a été décernée, revient une place centrale parmi les moments heureux de cette longue vie.

Annexe / Appendix

Photographies de l'évènement/Photographies of the Event

Katharina Boele-Woelki, Hein D. Kötz

K. Boele-Woelki, D. P. Fernàndez Arroyo (eds.), *The Past, Present and Future of Comparative Law - Le passé, le présent et le futur du droit comparé*, Ius Comparatum – Global Studies in Comparative Law 29, https://doi.org/10.1007/978-3-319-93770-0

Rodolfo Sacco, Antonio Gambaro, Marek Safjan, Jean-Louis Baudouin, Marta Cartabia, Hein D. Kötz, Bénédicte Fauvarque-Cosson, Attila Harmathy, Xavier Blanc-Jouvan

Jean-Louis Baudouin, Marek Safjan

Hein D. KÖTZ, Bénédicte FAUVARQUE-COSSON

Attila HARMATHY, Xavier BLANC-JOUVAN

Mary Ann Glendon, Jean-Louis Baudouin, Katharina Boele-Woelki

Rodolfo Sacco, Katharina Boele-Woelki, Diego P. Fernández Arroyo

Antonio GAMBARO

Diego P. FERNÁNDEZ ARROYO, Katharina BOELE-WOELKI, Hein D. KÖTZ

Hein D. Kötz, Katharina Boele-Woelki, Diego P. Fernández Arroyo

Bénédicte Fauvarque-Cosson, Katharina Boele-Woelki, Diego P. Fernández Arroyo

Diego P. FERNÁNDEZ ARROYO,Katharina BOELE-WOELKI, Xavier BLANC-JOUVAN

Rodolfo SACCO, Antonio GAMBARO, Xavier BLANC-JOUVAN,
Hein D. KÖTZ, Mary Ann GLENDON, Jean-Louis BAUDOUIN

Marta CARTABIA

Mary Ann GLENDON, Katharina BOELE-WOELKI

Bibliographie sélective/Selected Bibliography

Mary Ann Glendon

Glendon MA (1977) State, law and family: family law in transition in the United States and Western Europe. North-Holland Publishing Co., Amsterdam
Glendon MA (1981) The new family and the new property. Butterworths, Toronto
Glendon MA (1989a) Abortion and divorce in western law. Harvard University Press, Cambridge
Glendon MA (1989b) The transformation of family law. State, law, and family in the United States and Western Europe. The University of Chicago Press, Chicago
Glendon MA (1991) Rights talk: the impoverishment of political discourse. The Free Press, New York
Glendon MA (1996) A nation under lawyers. Harvard University Press, Cambridge
Glendon MA (2002) A world made new: Eleanor Roosevelt and the Universal Declaration of Human Rights. Random House, New York
Glendon MA (2006) Traditions in Turmoil. Sapientia Press of Ave Maria University, Ann Arbor
Glendon MA (2011) The forum and the tower: how scholars and politicians have imagined the world, from Plato to Eleanor Roosevelt. Oxford University Press, Oxford
Glendon MA, Alvira R (eds) (2014) Religion & civil society: the changing faces of religion & secularity. Georg Olms Verlag AG, Hildesheim
Glendon MA, Zacher H (eds) (2012) Universal rights in a world of diversity: the case of religious freedom. Pontifical Academy of Social Science, Vatican City
Glendon MA, Carozza PG, Picker CB (eds) (2015) Comparative legal traditions. Text, materials and cases on western law. West Publishing Co., St Paul

Hein D. Kötz

Kötz HD (1998) Vom Beitrag der Rechtsgeschichte zu den modernen Aufgaben der Rechtsvergleichung. In: Caroni/Dilcher (Hrsg.) Norm und Tradition, Welche Geschichtlichkeit für die Rechtsgeschichte? (Köln), pp 153–168
Kötz HD (1999) Comparative law in Germany today. Rev.int.dr.comp.:753–768
Kötz HD (2002) Alte und neue Aufgaben der Rechtsvergleichung. JZ:257–264

K. Boele-Woelki, D. P. Fernàndez Arroyo (eds.), *The Past, Present and Future of Comparative Law - Le passé, le présent et le futur du droit comparé*, Ius Comparatum – Global Studies in Comparative Law 29, https://doi.org/10.1007/978-3-319-93770-0

Kötz HD (2005a) In: Basedow J, Hopt K, Zimmermann R (eds) Undogmatisches, Rechtsvergleichende und rechtsökonomische Studien aus 30 Jahren. Mohr Siebeck

Kötz HD (2005b) Der Einfluss des Common Law auf die internationale Vertragspraxis. Festschrift für Andreas Heldrich:771–780

Kötz HD (2012a) Vertragsrecht, 2nd edn. Mohr Siebeck

Kötz HD (2012b) Contract law in Europe and the United States: legal unification in the civil law and common law. Tulane Eur Civil Law Forum 27:1–16

Kötz HD (2017) European contract law, 2nd edn (trans: Weir T, Mertens G). Oxford University Press

Kötz HD (1998) Towards a European Civil Code: contracts for the benefit of third parties. In: Institute of Comparative Law in Japan (ed) Toward comparative law in the 21st century. Chuo University Press, Tokyo, pp 115–136

Kötz HD, Wagner G (2016) Deliktsrecht, 13th edn. Academia Iuris (translated into Japanese)

Kötz HD, Zweigert K (1998) Introduction to comparative law, 3rd edn (trans: Weir T, also translated into Chinese, Japanese, Korean, Italian, Russian, Latvian). Oxford University Press

Xavier Blanc-Jouvan

Blanc-Jouvan X (1957) Les rapports collectifs de travail aux États-Unis. Dalloz, Paris

Blanc-Jouvan X (1964) Les droits fonciers collectifs dans les coutumes malgaches. Revue internationale de droit comparé 16(2):333–368

Blanc-Jouvan X (1975) Le rôle international d'une revue de droit comparé. Revue internationale de droit comparé 27(1):57–71

Blanc-Jouvan X (1988) Réflexions sur l'enseignement du droit comparé. Revue internationale de droit comparé 40(4):751–763

Blanc-Jouvan X (1990) La flexibilité du temps de travail. Revue internationale de droit comparé 42 (2):693–724

Blanc-Jouvan X (1993) L'enseignement du droit national aux étudiants étrangers. Revue internationale de droit comparé 48(1):9–26

Blanc-Jouvan X (1996) La formation au droit comparé, Le point de vue d'un universitaire. Revue internationale de droit comparé 48(2):347–367

Blanc-Jouvan X (2000) Prologue, L'Avenir du droit comparé. Société de législation comparée, Paris, pp 7–15

Jean-Louis Baudouin

Baudouin J-L (1963) Secret professionnel et droit au secret dans le droit de la preuve, Paris 1965, Librairie générale de droit et de jurisprudence. Prix de thèse de la faculté de droit de l'Université de Paris

Baudouin J-L (1986) Family relations in modern medicine: a Canadian perspective, dans Actes du XIIe congrès International de droit comparé, Montréal, p 256

Baudouin J-L (1987) Produire l'homme: de quel droit? en collaboration avec Catherine Labrusse, Paris, P.U.F.

Baudouin J-L (1991) Medicine, biomedical innovation and the law in Canada. In: Roy DJ, Safjan M, Dybowski T (eds) Medicine ethics and maw: Canadian and Polish perspectives. The Center for Bioethics, Clinical Research Center of Montreal

Baudouin J-L (1994) Vie et mort de la personne: La personne humaine en droit compare: apparition et disparition, Rapport des 4è Journées René Savatier, université de Poitiers, Presses universitaires de France, p 73
Baudouin J-L (1997a) Bioéthique: de l'éthique au droit, du droit à l'éthique, in Actes du Colloque international, Lausanne, 17-18 oct 1996, publ. de l'Institut Suisse de droit comparé
Baudouin J-L (1997b) De l'éthique au droit, du droit à l'éthique. Rapport de synthèse, in Actes du colloque international de bioéthique, publ. de l'Institut suisse de droit comparé, vol 30, p 205
Baudouin J-L (1998) La vérité et le droit des personnes: aspects nouveaux, 1987, 18 R.D.G. p 801; aussi dans Travaux de l'Association Henri Capitant, Paris, Economica, T. XXXVIII
Baudouin J-L (2001) Justice et équilibre: la nouvelle moralité contractuelle du droit civil québécois, in Études offertes à Jacques Ghestin – Le contrat au début du XXIè siècle, Paris, L.G.D.J, p 29 à 44
Baudouin J-L (2005) Les obligations, 6eme ed., en collaboration avec Pierre-Gabriel Jobin et Nathalie Vezina, Cowansville, Editions Yvon Blais
Baudouin J-L (2009–2010) Rapport de synthèse de Journées Suisses de l'Association Henri Capitant [2009–2010] 40 R.D.U. 365
Baudouin J-L (2013) L'abus de droit d'ester en justice, valse hésitation entre le législateur et le juge, dans Mélanges Camille Jauffret, Paris, Dalloz, p 53
Baudouin J-L (2014a) La responsabilité civile, 8eme ed., en collaboration avec Patrice Deslauriers et Benoît Moore, Cowansville, Éditions Yvon Blais
Baudouin J-L (2014b) Responsabilité civile comparée: droit civil et common law, 48 R.J.T. p 683 (Revue juridique Thémis de l'Université de Montréal)
Baudouin J-L (2015) The law of civil responsibility in Quebec. International Encyclopaedia of Comparative Law, Kluwer, 1998, 2010, 2013

Rodolfo Sacco

Sacco R (1949) La buona fede. Memorie dell'Istituto Giuridico, Torino
Sacco R (1968) La proprietà. Giappichelli, Torino
Sacco R (1981) L'arricchimento ottenuto mediante fatto ingiusto, UTET, Torino, 1959; réimpression, ESI, Napoli
Sacco R (1991a) La comparaison juridique au service de la connaissance du droit. Economica, Paris
Sacco R (1991b) Legal formants: a dynamic approach to comparative law. Am J Comp Law XXXIX:1–34/343–402
Sacco R (1992) Introduzione al diritto comparato, 5 e éd. UTET, Torino
Sacco R (1996) Sistemi giuridici comparati. UTET, Torino
Sacco R (2001a) Le droit de l'occident et d'ailleurs, L.G.D.J., L'extenso, Paris, (avec Gambaro et Vogel)
Sacco R (2001b) Einführung in die Rechtsvergleichung. Nomos Verlagsgesellschaft, Badenbaden
Sacco R (2001c) Introduçâo ao Direito Comparado. Editora Revista dos Tribunais, Sâo Paulo
Sacco R (2003) Il concetto di interpretazione del diritto, Memorie dell'Istituto Giuridico, Torino, 1947; réimpression, Giapplichelli, Torino
Sacco R (2005) Il Fatto, l'atto, il negozio. UTET, Torino
Sacco R (2007) Antropologia giuridica. Il Mulino, Bologna
Sacco R (2009a) Il diritto africano, UTET, Torino, 1995; Le droit africain, Dalloz, Paris,
Sacco R (2009b) Anthropologie juridique. Dalloz, Paris
Sacco R (2013) Antropologia jurídica. Editora WMF Martins Fontes, Sâo Paulo
Sacco R (2014) Il possesso, 1e éd., Giuffré, Milano, 1988; 3e éd., Giuffré, Milano, (avec R. Caterina)
Sacco R (2015) Il diritto muto. Il Mulino, Bologna
Sacco R (2016a) El derecho mudo. Communitas, Lima
Sacco R (2016b) Il contratto, 1e éd, UTET, Torino, 1975; 4e éd, UTET, Torino, (avec G. De Nova)

MIX
Papier aus verantwortungsvollen Quellen
Paper from responsible sources
FSC® C105338

If you have any concerns about our products,
you can contact us on
ProductSafety@springernature.com

In case Publisher is established outside the EU,
the EU authorized representative is:
Springer Nature Customer Service Center GmbH
Europaplatz 3, 69115 Heidelberg, Germany

Printed by Libri Plureos GmbH
in Hamburg, Germany